THE **IRISH PUB** COOKBOOK

THE **IRISH PUB** COOKBOOK

BY Margaret M. Johnson

PHOTOGRAPHS BY Margaret M. Johnson

FOOD PHOTOGRAPHS BY Leigh Beisch

CHRONICLE BOOKS

SAN FRANCISCO

The recipes for Bacon, Blue Cheese, and Courgette Soup (page 58) and Bibb, Bacon, and Apple Salad with Camembert Dressing (page 77) are adapted with the permission of Bord Bia (Irish Food Board). The recipe for Warm Scallop Salad with Cider Dressing (page 88) is adapted with the permission of Magners Irish Cider.

Photo credits: pages 22–23, courtesy of Johnnie Fox's Pub; page 92, courtesy of Shannon Development.

Library of Congress Cataloging-in-Publication Data available.

ISBN-10: 0-8118-4485-4

ISBN-13: 978-0-8118-4485-7

Manufactured in China.

Designed *by* Ayako Akazawa

Prop styling *by* Sara Slavin

Food styling *by* Sandra Cook

Food stylist assistants Penny Zweidinger *and* Elisabet der Nederlanden

Photo assistant Angelica Cao

Typesetting *by* Janis Reed

The photographer wishes to thank the stupendous photo team of Sara, Sandra, Angelica, Shashona, Penny, and Elisabet. It is always a pleasure working with such a creative, fun group. I would also like to thank Chronicle Books for another fun assignment, and mostly Ayako Akazawa for working with us and supporting our efforts in this interesting project.

Distributed in Canada *by* Raincoast Books
9050 Shaughnessy Street
Vancouver, British Columbia V6P 6E5

10 9 8 7 6 5 4 3 2

Chronicle Books LLC
85 Second Street
San Francisco, California 94105

www.chroniclebooks.com

For my husband, Carl, and my son, Mark,
who have never met a pub they didn't like.

ACKNOWLEDGMENTS

I'd like to express my thanks to the Irish publicans and chefs who contributed recipes and advice for this book, especially members of Irish Pubs of Distinction; Cian Molloy, author of *The Story of the Irish Pub;* Bord Bia (Irish Food Board), in Dublin and Chicago; Orla Carey of Tourism Ireland; Gerry Lennon of Belfast Visitor and Convention Bureau; the McNally Design Group and the Irish Pub Company, in Dublin; the Galway Oyster Festival committee; the James Joyce Centre, Dublin; Roger Wort of Ulster Magazines, Ltd., in Belfast; Caroline Workman of Foodstuff Ireland, in Belfast; the Edward Dillon Company, in Dublin; and Roisin Hennerty and Molly O'Loughlin of the Irish Dairy Board, in Chicago. Thanks also to Erin Crawford, Renée Erhardt, and Kate Schumacher for assistance with recipe testing; and to Madeleine Morel, my agent, who continues to provide guidance and encouragement. Thanks go to Bill LeBlond, senior editor, Chronicle Books, for his faith in me again, and to Amy Treadwell, for her editorial assistance. Finally, heartfelt thanks to my husband, Carl, for his continued indulgence in all things Irish!

TABLE OF CONTENTS

•••••
DEBARRA FOLK CLUB, CLONAKILTY, COUNTY CORK

"A good puzzle," mused Leopold Bloom,
"would be to cross Dublin without passing a pub."
—*James Joyce's* Ulysses

The pub, short for "public house," is one of Ireland's most beloved institutions. There are an estimated 11,000 pubs in the Republic of Ireland, 1,650 in Northern Ireland, and more than 1,000 in Dublin alone. These licensed premises—part clubhouse, part town hall, part church—have served for years as venues for social events, sporting news, local gossip, music sessions, literary soirées, real estate deals, political debates, revolutionary plots, and, lest we forget, for knocking back a pint of Guinness or a "ball of malt," also known as a glass of whiskey.

Public houses date back to medieval taverns, coaching inns, and shebeens—illegal drinking dens that flourished under colonial rule. In Victorian times, brewing and distilling were major industries in Ireland, and many city pubs, especially those in Dublin, Cork, and Galway, still retain their mahogany and marble counters, carved woodwork, gaslights, and period mirrors. The Crown Liquor Saloon, in Belfast, architecturally distinguished with its stained and painted glass, plasterwork ceiling, marbling, and mosaics, is so revered that it's even a member of Britain's National Trust!

A rural Irish pub might be an extension of the village shop, or it might serve as the local post office or, in the case of a pub in Wexford, an extension of a funeral parlor; many traditional ones still feature intimate, partitioned booths or cubicles called "snugs," and others have boldly painted or black-and-white beamed exteriors with thatched roofs.

Regardless of design, Irish pubs are perhaps the best expressions of Irish life and culture and are true keepers of the spirit of the land. No visit to Ireland is complete without at least a visit to one to see firsthand how a barman draws a proper pint of Guinness; to experience the *craic* (pronounced "crack"), the Irish expression for fun; and, of course, to sample the food the country is renowned for—pub grub.

Long before Michelin began anointing Irish chefs with stars and red M's, pub grub—simple sandwiches, thick soups, hearty stews, jacket potatoes, salad plates, and big joints of meat sliced at the carvery—was considered to be the quintessential Irish food. Writing about it twenty years ago, tourism expert Arthur Frommer commented: "The Irish never were great eaters. *Big* eaters, yes, *gourmets*, no. Potatoes and buttermilk were the great staples before the Famine, and even in current, more prosperous times, the Irish have prided themselves on being meat- and potato people—'nothing fancy'—with a great taste for thick slabs of brown bread and apple tart."

What Frommer was talking about was pub grub, hearty food that despite its apparent simplicity has developed into a cuisine in its own right. The term "gastropub" was recently coined in the United Kingdom to describe those pubs that turn out good meals as easily as they pour good drinks. Much like a French bistro or an Italian trattoria, where natives gather for unpretentious and hearty food, the Irish pub (of which there are thousands worldwide) is, undoubtedly, the country's leading exponent of good-value meals, hospitality, and tradition.

From Davy Byrnes in Dublin to Kehoe's Pub and Parlour in Kilmore Quay, and from Durty Nelly's in Bunratty to Grace Neill's in Donaghadee, you'll find traditional country-style cooking along with a few surprises. You've come to expect bacon and cabbage, shepherd's pie, seafood chowder, and apple tarts, and now you'll be delighted by salads spiced with Asian dressings, tortes filled with cheeses and sun-dried tomatoes, risottos topped with basil or black pudding, and cheesecakes marbled with Irish cream and stout. The best part: you can easily make these at home. *The Irish Pub Cookbook* transports these dishes into your kitchen in seven chapters, each with photos, history, folklore, and "blackboard specials" from some of the country's most famous licensed premises.

In *The Story of the Irish Pub,* author Cian Molloy says, "The Irish pub is part of a living tradition; it is part of our unique culture and it deserves to be cherished and celebrated." Spice it up with some serious cooking, and it's no wonder the pub is such a beloved institution.

Sláinte agus go marfaidh sibh an céad. "Good health and may you outlive one hundred years!"

CHAPTER I

STARTERS

Originally, an appetizer, or "starter" as it's called in Ireland, was confined to the realm of soup or salad—a small portion of food to whet one's appetite before the main meal was served. In most households, however, one course, and only one course, was served, and the practice of offering "something to start" was reserved for more affluent Irish families or for restaurants. When the idea of several courses, or "removes" as they were called in ancient times, entered the dining scene, the first course was generally something simple, such as potted fish, poultry, or meat; smoked salmon; raw or fried oysters; cooked prawns with sauce; or some type of cheese. Today's restaurant and pub starters are in the same vein, with variations of potted meat or pâté, steamed seafood, and cheese dishes among the most popular offerings.

The Brazen Head, on Lower Bridge Street, in Dublin, has been trading for 800 years. It is reputed to be not only the oldest pub in Dublin, but also one of the oldest pubs in all of Ireland. It stands on the site of a twelfth-century tavern near the River Liffey, and started serving the public before Ireland's first licensing laws were passed in 1635. Like many inns of that era, it had a courtyard for catering to visiting coaches and rooms for overnight accommodation, and like many humble Irish establishments, good food and wine. Merchants, smugglers, rebels, and patriots were counted as patrons of the Brazen Head, including leading figures in Ireland's independence movement, such as Robert Emmet, Wolfe Tone, and Daniel O'Connell. No longer a hotel, the Brazen Head remains one of Dublin's most distinctive public houses and has an enviable reputation for providing good food and drink, traditional Irish music, and lively conversation. These mussels, steamed in garlic and Guinness, are one of the pub's most popular starters. **SERVES 4**

Mussels in
GARLIC AND GUINNESS

2 pounds fresh mussels, scrubbed, debearded, and rinsed in cold water

1 shallot, minced

3 cloves garlic, minced

1 tablespoon minced fresh flat-leaf parsley, plus extra for garnish

1½ teaspoons minced fresh thyme

½ cup Guinness

½ cup half-and-half

2 tablespoons unsalted Kerrygold Irish butter

Lemon wedges for serving

French bread for serving

1 Put a stockpot or Dutch oven over medium heat. When the pot is hot, add the mussels and remaining ingredients and cover immediately. (The mussels will make a sizzling sound.) Cook, stirring once or twice, for 6 to 8 minutes, or until the mussels open. Discard any that do not open.

2 To serve, divide the mussels among shallow bowls and ladle the broth over them. Sprinkle with parsley and serve with a wedge of lemon and slices of bread to sop up the juice.

Prawns, which are the equivalent of jumbo shrimp, are found on virtually every pub menu in Ireland. They're served simply on a bed of mixed salad greens with a cocktail sauce known as Marie Rose sauce and a few slices of brown soda bread (pages 95 and 98). Make the sauce at least an hour before you plan to serve it. SERVES 4

PRAWN COCKTAIL
with Marie Rose Sauce

MARIE ROSE SAUCE
2 tablespoons heavy (whipping) cream
2 tablespoons mayonnaise
2 tablespoons ketchup
Dash of Worcestershire sauce
1 teaspoon fresh lemon juice
1 teaspoon sherry
Salt and freshly ground pepper to taste

4 ounces mixed salad greens
24 prawns or jumbo shrimp, cooked and
  peeled
Lemon wedges for serving
Minced fresh flat-leaf parsley for garnish

1. **To make the sauce:** In a small bowl, whip the cream with an electric mixer until soft peaks form. Whisk in the remaining ingredients. Refrigerate for 1 hour.

2. To serve, divide the mixed greens among 4 salad plates. Arrange 6 prawns on top of each serving and drizzle with the sauce. Serve with a lemon wedge and sprinkle with parsley.

CELEBRATING SEAFOOD IN GALWAY AND CORK

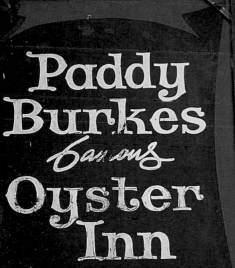

The Irish are very celebratory when it comes to food, especially with the arrival of the first oysters of the season in September, after their long nap through late spring and summer, and the beginning of the mussel harvest in May.

Two locations in County Galway—Clarenbridge and Galway City—host three-day extravaganzas honoring the oyster, which include shucking contests and black-tie balls. The residents of Clarenbridge (nine miles south of Galway), who proclaim, "the world is your oyster and Clarenbridge its home," have held their festival on the first or second weekend of September since 1954. This weekend of *craic* (Irish for "good times") includes cooking demonstrations, oyster-opening competitions, and seafood luncheons held under a festival marquee around Paddy Burkes Oyster Inn. But the festivities also spread to the pubs and restaurants throughout the village: Moran's, Raftery's Rest, O'Donaghue's, Sherry's, and Jordan's bars among them. The traditional accompaniment for the oyster fare is Murphy's, a County Cork–brewed stout produced by the main sponsor.

Also founded in 1954, the Galway International Oyster Festival, sponsored by Guinness, takes place on the last weekend of September, undoubtedly to allow a sufficient time for locals to recuperate from the Clarenbridge bash. The word "Guinness" precedes the name of most events at the fest, since the company hosts many of them, including the international oyster-opening championship, which draws aficionados from all over the world. Guinness also supplies libations at events held under the festival marquee pitched at the historic Spanish Arch and along the pub trail throughout the city. Music, parades, an "elegant lady" competition, receptions, brunches, and balls add to the general revelry. During the festival weeks, more than 10,000 people converge on these two Galway venues, and an estimated 40,000 oysters are consumed. No one keeps track of the pints!

On a slightly smaller, but no less boisterous, scale, a mussel festival takes place in Bantry, Country Cork, during the first weekend in May. Here it's nonstop mussels, Murphy's, and merrymaking when a similar round of events pays homage to the local shellfish. For details, see Resources, page 214.

. . . .

PADDY BURKES OYSTER INN, CLARENBRIDGE, COUNTY GALWAY

The O'Crowley family has operated An Súgán in Clonakilty, County Cork, for more than twenty-five years. As the locality has grown, so, too, has An Súgán, a popular spot for tourists and locals alike. Situated in the scenic region of West Cork, the pub offers a traditional menu with innovative additions made with local ingredients. The pier in Ring, a short distance from town, provides the "catch of the day," like this salmon dish, which is served with an herby wine sauce. SERVES 4

SALMON CAKES
with Dill and Wine Sauce

SALMON CAKES

1 pound salmon fillets, poached (see Note)

2 tablespoons minced fresh chives

1 teaspoon minced fresh ginger

3 tablespoons sweet pickle relish

⅓ cup mayonnaise

Salt and freshly ground pepper to taste

2 large eggs

½ cup milk

All-purpose flour for dredging

Fresh white bread crumbs for dredging (see Note, page 33)

Canola oil for frying

DILL AND WINE SAUCE

1 tablespoon unsalted Kerrygold Irish butter

⅓ cup minced shallots

1 cup dry white wine

¾ cup homemade fish stock (page 62) or bottled clam juice

¾ cup heavy (whipping) cream

Freshly ground pepper to taste

2 tomatoes, plunged in boiling water for about 15 seconds, peeled, quartered, seeded, and chopped

1 tablespoon minced fresh dill

Mixed salad greens for garnish

1. **To start the salmon cakes:** With a fork, flake the salmon in a medium bowl. Stir in the chives, ginger, relish, and mayonnaise. Season with salt and pepper.

2. With floured hands, shape the mixture into four 3-inch cakes. In a small bowl, whisk together the eggs and milk. Put the flour in a shallow dish. Dredge each cake in the flour, then in the egg wash, and then coat in bread crumbs. Refrigerate for 1 hour.

3. **Meanwhile, make the sauce:** In a small skillet over medium heat, melt the butter. Cook the shallots for 3 to 5 minutes, or until tender but not browned. Add the wine and cook for 5 to 8 minutes, or until reduced by half. Add the fish stock or clam juice and cook for 5 to 8 minutes, or until reduced by half. Add the cream and cook for 3 to 5 minutes, or until the sauce is smooth. Season with pepper. Pass the sauce through a fine sieve. Return to the pan and stir in the tomatoes and dill. Keep warm over low heat.

4. In a large skillet over medium heat, warm the oil. Fry the salmon cakes for 3 to 5 minutes on each side, or until golden.

5. To serve, put a salmon cake in the center of each of 4 salad plates and garnish with mixed greens. Drizzle with some of the sauce and pass the rest.

NOTE: *To poach the salmon, combine 1 cup of dry white wine and 1 cup of water in a large skillet over medium heat. Heat to just below boiling, then add the salmon fillets, a few peppercorns, 1 sprig of fresh flat-leaf parsley, and a pinch of salt. Cover and cook gently for 12 to 15 minutes, or until the salmon flakes when pierced with a fork. With a slotted spoon, transfer the fish to a plate and let cool.*

Johnnie Fox's, one of the country's most famous pubs, is reputedly the highest pub in Ireland, sitting as it does in the Dublin mountain village of Glencullen. Altitude aside, the pub, founded in 1798, is filled to the rafters with historic photos, memorabilia, bric-a-brac, and antique furniture and could easily pass as a folk museum. The pub has won many awards for its good food, especially for its seafood platters. The proprietors like to boast that "nobody goes away hungry or thirsty." Its smoked salmon dishes are among the most popular. This pâté, which the chef rolls into a log shape, can also be served in small ramekins. **SERVES 4**

SMOKED SALMON PÂTÉ

8 ounces Irish oak-smoked salmon or similar smoked salmon

½ cup (1 stick) unsalted Kerrygold Irish butter at room temperature

2 tablespoons cream cheese at room temperature

1½ tablespoons fresh lemon juice

2 teaspoons prepared tartar sauce

2 teaspoons prepared horseradish

2 teaspoons port

Pinch of cayenne pepper

2 tablespoons minced fresh chives

1 tablespoon freshly ground pepper

1 tablespoon minced fresh dill

5 ounces mixed salad greens

Chopped red onions for garnish (optional)

Cumberland sauce (page 28) for serving

Brown soda bread (pages 95 and 98) for serving

1   In a food processor or blender, combine the salmon, butter, cream cheese, lemon juice, tartar sauce, horseradish, port, and cayenne pepper. Process for 20 to 30 seconds, or until smooth.

2   With a rubber spatula, spread out the salmon mixture on a 12-inch-long piece of wax paper to about a 1-inch thickness. Sprinkle with the chives and pepper. Using the wax paper to help you, roll up the mixture to form a log. Refrigerate for 1 to 2 hours, or until firm. Scatter the dill on a plate. Remove the log from the refrigerator and roll it in the dill.

3   To serve, divide the mixed greens among 4 salad plates. Cut the log into 1-inch-thick slices and place them on the greens. Sprinkle with onions, if using, and drizzle with Cumberland sauce. Serve with brown soda bread.

While oysters and clams are usually offered on American menus "on the half shell" with cocktail sauce, you're more likely to find them less adorned in Irish pubs, with only a wedge of lemon or a spoonful of mignonette sauce. The less-is-more theory allows the real flavor of these crustaceous delights to take center stage, as it does in famous oyster pubs in County Galway like Paddy Burkes in Clarenbridge, and Moran's Oyster Cottage, at the Weir, in Kilcolgan. **SERVES 4**

OYSTERS
with Mignonette Sauce

24 fresh oysters, shucked

MIGNONETTE SAUCE
1 cup red wine vinegar (not balsamic)
½ cup minced fresh shallots
1 teaspoon freshly ground black pepper
1 tablespoon minced fresh flat-leaf parsley
Pinch of salt

Brown soda bread (pages 95 and 98) for serving (optional)

1 Shuck the oysters (see Note), and leave each one in the deep half of the shell. Discard the other half. Make a bed of finely crushed ice in each of 4 four shallow bowls, arrange 6 oysters on top, and refrigerate.

2 **To make the sauce:** Combine all the ingredients in a small lidded jar, cover, and shake to blend. Let stand for 15 minutes.

3 To serve, spoon the sauce into 4 small ramekins or bowls and place in the center of the oysters. Serve with a few slices of brown soda bread, if desired.

NOTE: *To shuck oysters, scrub thoroughly with a stiff brush under cold running water. Wearing heavy rubber gloves, insert the tip of an oyster knife between the halves of the shell just behind the hinge or muscle. Cut through the muscle. Lift off the shallow shell. Loosen the oyster from the bottom shell with the point of the knife.*
• • • • •
FOLLOWING PAGES: JOHNNIE FOX'S PUB, GLENCULLEN, COUNTY DUBLIN

Paddy Burkes, also known as the Oyster Inn, is a picturesque roadside pub in Clarenbridge, County Galway. Complete with partitions, wood-lined snugs, turn-of-the-century bric-a-brac, and old photographs, the pub is also the centerpiece of the annual oyster festival, first celebrated here in September 1954 (see page 17). Oysters are one of the most requested dishes in the pub. The chef prepares them Florentine style with spinach and cheese, and in this garlicky version, which is everyone's favorite. SERVES 4

OYSTERS
Baked with Garlic and Herbs

24 fresh oysters

Kosher or rock salt as needed

½ cup (1 stick) unsalted Kerrygold Irish butter

¼ cup minced shallots

2 cups fresh white bread crumbs (see Note, page 33)

¼ cup fresh lemon juice

Salt and freshly ground pepper to taste

½ cup (1 stick) Kerrygold Garlic and Herb Butter, or a homemade equivalent (see Note)

Lemon wedges for serving

1   Shuck the oysters (see Note on page 21), and leave each one in the deep half of the shell. Discard the other half shell. Arrange the oysters in a baking sheet spread with kosher or rock salt (to balance the shells). Preheat the oven to 375°F.

2   In a large skillet over medium heat, melt the unsalted butter. Add the shallots and cook for 2 to 3 minutes, or until soft. Stir in the bread crumbs, lemon juice, salt, and pepper. Spoon some of the crumb mixture over each oyster and top with a teaspoonful of the garlic and herb butter. Bake for 12 to 15 minutes, or until the crumbs are golden.

3   **To serve,** place 6 oysters on each of 4 serving plates and garnish with a lemon wedge.

NOTE: *Kerrygold's Garlic and Herb Butter is a new addition to the company's line of dairy products. It's sold in 4-ounce sticks. If you can't find it in your area or prefer to make your own, mix 1 tablespoon of minced garlic and 1 tablespoon of minced fresh flat-leaf parsley with 1 stick of softened unsalted butter.*

Pâtés are popular pub fare, whether they're made with chicken or duck livers, game, or smoked fish. They're generally served with slices of warm buttered toast and piquant relishes or sauces, such as red onion marmalade or Cumberland sauce (see page 28). At the lively Errigle Inn on Ormeau Road, in Belfast, where this recipe originated, the chef prefers marmalade. He suggests you make it at least a day in advance to let the flavors meld: it will keep for several days refrigerated. Both the marmalade and Cumberland sauce are delicious with cold meats and with a Ploughman's Lunch (page 80). The Errigle Inn is a member of Irish Pubs of Distinction (see page 159). **SERVES 8; MAKES 2 CUPS OF MARMALADE**

CHICKEN LIVER PÂTÉ
with Red Onion Marmalade

RED ONION MARMALADE
4 tablespoons unsalted Kerrygold Irish butter
¼ cup sugar
4 medium red onions, thinly sliced
2 tablespoons port
1 sprig fresh thyme

PÂTÉ
1½ pounds chicken livers, rinsed and trimmed
¼ cup brandy
¼ cup port

Salt and freshly ground pepper to taste
1 cup (2 sticks) plus 2 tablespoons unsalted Kerrygold Irish butter
1 onion, finely chopped
4 cloves garlic, minced
3 or 4 sprigs fresh thyme
½ cup heavy (whipping) cream
2 large eggs

Mixed salad greens for garnish
Toast or French bread for serving

1 **To make the marmalade:** In a large skillet over medium heat, melt the butter. Stir in the sugar and cook for 5 to 7 minutes, or until the butter starts to brown. Add the onions, port, and thyme and cook, covered, over low heat for 15 to 20 minutes, or until the onions are wilted and caramelized. Transfer to a small bowl and let cool completely. Cover and refrigerate for at least 2 hours and up to 5 days.

2   **To start the pâté:** In a large bowl, combine the chicken livers, brandy, port, salt, and pepper. Cover and refrigerate for 12 hours.

3   Preheat the oven to 325°F. Butter an 8-by-4-by-3-inch loaf pan or a small terrine, and line it with a piece of parchment paper long enough to cover the top of the pâté.

4   **To finish the pâté:** In a small skillet over medium heat, melt the 2 tablespoons of butter. Add the onion, garlic, and thyme and cook for 3 to 4 minutes, or until the vegetables are soft but not browned. Remove from the heat and let cool. Discard the thyme. Melt the remaining 1 cup of butter in a small saucepan and let cool.

5   In a food processor or blender, combine the chicken liver mixture, onion mixture, melted butter, cream, and eggs. Process for 15 to 20 seconds, or until smooth. Spoon the mixture into the prepared pan or terrine, cover with the parchment paper, and place in a baking pan. Add enough hot water to come halfway up the sides of the terrine. Bake for 1 to 1$^1/_4$ hours, or until the top is slightly firm to the touch. Remove from the oven and transfer to a wire rack. Let cool completely. Peel back the parchment paper from the top, invert the pâté onto a platter, and peel off the remaining paper. Wrap with plastic wrap and refrigerate for 4 to 6 hours, or overnight.

6   **To serve,** cut the pâté into 1-inch-thick slices and garnish with some mixed greens. Serve with the red onion marmalade and buttered toast or slices of French bread.

St. Killian is the best known of the Carrigbyrne Farmhouse Cheese Company's Camembert-style cheeses. Made near Enniscorthy, County Wexford, it is easily recognized by its hexagonal shape. Like other white rind cheeses, St. Killian is delicious deep-fried in beer batter and served with tangy Cumberland sauce or cranberry Cumberland sauce (see variation), both of which should be prepared a day in advance to let the flavors meld. A version of this recipe will be found on nearly every pub menu in Ireland. **SERVES 4; MAKES ABOUT 1½ CUPS OF CUMBERLAND SAUCE**

DEEP-FRIED ST. KILLIAN CHEESE
with Cumberland Sauce

CUMBERLAND SAUCE

2 oranges

1 lemon

5 tablespoons port

One 10-ounce jar red currant jelly

½ teaspoon ground ginger

1 teaspoon dry mustard

FRIED ST. KILLIAN CHEESE

¾ cup all-purpose flour

½ cup flat beer at room temperature

Pinch of salt

1 teaspoon canola oil

1 large egg, separated, at room temperature

Two 8-ounce rounds Camembert, preferably St. Killian

Canola oil for frying

Mixed salad greens for garnish

1   **To make the Cumberland sauce:** With a vegetable peeler, peel the zest off the oranges and lemon. With a sharp knife, shred as thinly as possible. Put the zest into a small saucepan and cover with cold water. Bring to a boil, then reduce the heat and simmer for 5 minutes, or until the zest starts to soften. Drain and set aside.

CONTINUED

2   Squeeze the juice from the oranges and lemon into a small saucepan. Add the port, jelly, ginger, and mustard, and bring to a boil. Cook for 5 minutes, then reduce the heat and simmer for 10 minutes more, or until the mixture is reduced by half. Transfer the sauce to a small bowl and stir in the reserved zest. Refrigerate for at least 24 hours and up to 3 weeks.

3   **To make the fried cheese:** In a large bowl, whisk together the flour, beer, salt, and oil. There will be a few small lumps. Cover the bowl with plastic wrap and let stand in a warm place for about 3 hours. Stir in the egg yolk. In a small bowl, beat the egg white with an electric mixer until stiff peaks form. Fold into the beer batter.

4   Cut each round of cheese, rind and all, into 8 pie-shaped slices, then cut each slice crosswise in half. In an electric skillet, heat about 2 inches of oil to 325°F. Dip the cheese pieces, one at a time, into the beer batter. Drop into the hot oil, and cook in batches, turning as necessary with a wooden spoon, for 1 to 2 minutes, or until golden brown. With a slotted spoon, remove each piece as soon as it's browned, and drain on paper towels.

5   To serve, spoon the Cumberland sauce into 4 small ramekins or dishes and place each one in the center of a salad plate. Arrange the mixed greens around the ramekin and place 8 pieces of cheese on top of the greens.

VARIATION:

Cranberry Cumberland Sauce

Add 1 cup of fresh cranberries along with the port, jelly, ginger, and mustard and proceed with the recipe.

SUPERLATIVE PUBS

Oldest, highest, longest, smallest—many of Ireland's more well-known pubs make claims that add both charm and character to their premises.

Grace Neill's (see pages 86–87, 172), on High Street in Donaghadee, County Down, is officially listed as "the oldest bar in Ireland" in *The Guinness Book of Records*. Almost four centuries ago, in 1611, the Kings Arms first opened its doors for business in the seaside town of Donaghadee. Today, operating as Grace Neill's, it's firmly established as both a popular tourist destination and one of the most affable establishments in Ireland. The charming front bar is almost exactly as it was in the days of Grace Neill, its former innkeeper. The beams are constructed from the timbers of old ships, two snugs are filled with antique glass and stone bottles, a photo of its namesake hangs on a wall, and other turn-of-the-century memorabilia is scattered around. Beyond the original stone-floored pub is a library pub and stylish new restaurant featuring a pleasant mix of Southeast Asian and traditional Irish cuisine.

Also in contention for the title of "the oldest pub in Ireland" is the Brazen Head, on Lower Bridge Street, in Dublin (see page 14). While an inn has been on the site since the late twelfth century, the present structure dates only from 1668, possibly accounting for the challenge from Grace Neill's. It is definitely, however, the oldest pub in Dublin.

Other superlative pubs include the Purty Kitchen, on Old Dunleary Road, in Monkstown, the second-oldest in Dublin but the oldest in Monkstown, County Dublin; Hole in the Wall, on Blackhorse Avenue, in Dublin, which claims to be the longest pub in the country; John Kavanagh, at Prospect Square, in Dublin, which claims to be the pub with the longest continuous family ownership; and Johnnie Fox's, set high in the Dublin Mountains, in Glencullen, which claims to be not only among the oldest, but "undoubtedly" the highest pub in Ireland as well (see page 20).

· · · ·

BEER GARDEN AT THE BRAZEN HEAD PUB, DUBLIN

At Oliver St. John Gogarty's on Fleet Street, in Dublin, you'll find the anecdotes on the menu as entertaining as the choices. While deciding on whether to have Seafood Molly Malone or Sackville Street Casserole, you can read about the famous Irish surgeon/poet/politician/raconteur/imbiber for whom the restaurant is named, and enjoy anecdotes on Temple Bar history as well. Esther Dunne was a nineteenth-century provisions dealer with a shop next door at No. 57. This original recipe, named in her honor, dates from the 1850s, and is usually served drizzled with warm cranberry sauce. You might wish to try it with Cranberry Cumberland Sauce (see page 30), which should be made at least a day in advance to let the flavors meld. The potato cake is also delicious as a side dish with meat or fish.

SERVES 4

Esther Dunne's
BACON-POTATO CAKE

8 ounces russet potatoes, peeled and cut into 2-inch pieces

3 tablespoons unsalted Kerrygold Irish butter

2 tablespoons warm milk

1 tablespoon mixed dried herbs, such as tarragon, thyme, and marjoram

2 tablespoons minced fresh flat-leaf parsley

1½ teaspoons ground nutmeg

Salt and freshly ground pepper to taste

2 streaky rashers (traditional Irish bacon; see page 53), chopped

2 leaves cabbage, finely chopped

All-purpose flour for dredging

1 large egg mixed with 1 tablespoon water

Fresh white bread crumbs for dredging (see Note)

Canola oil for frying

Mixed salad greens for garnish

Cranberry Cumberland Sauce (page 30) for serving (optional)

1   In a large saucepan, cook the potatoes in boiling salted water for 12 to 15 minutes, or until tender. Drain and mash. Re-cover and return to low heat for 2 to 3 minutes to dry out the potatoes. Remove from the heat, add the butter and milk, and stir until smooth. Stir in the dried herbs, parsley, nutmeg, salt, and pepper. Let cool for 5 to 8 minutes.

2   Meanwhile, in a small skillet over medium heat, cook the bacon for 3 to 4 minutes on each side, or until crisp. With a slotted spoon or spatula, transfer to paper towels to drain. Using the same skillet, cook the cabbage for 4 to 5 minutes, or until wilted. Stir the cabbage into the potatoes, crumble in the bacon, and stir until well blended. Shape the potato mixture into 4 evenly sized cakes. Put the flour in one shallow dish, the egg wash in another, and the bread crumbs in a third. Lightly dredge each cake in flour, dip in egg wash, then cover with bread crumbs.

3   In a large skillet over medium-high heat, heat the oil. Add the cakes and cook for 3 to 5 minutes on each side, or until browned. Serve immediately, or transfer to a baking sheet and keep warm in a preheated 300°F oven.

4   To serve, put a handful of mixed greens in the center of each of 4 salad plates and place 1 potato cake on top. If you like, spoon 1 to 2 tablespoons of sauce over it and pass the rest.

NOTE: *To make fresh bread crumbs, cut 5 to 6 slices of a stale baguette or rustic bread into ¹/₂-inch cubes. Put in a blender or a food processor fitted with a grating attachment. Process for 15 to 20 seconds, or until the mixture is ground into fine crumbs. Makes about 1 cup.*

Several Irish farmhouse cheese makers produce blue cheese: Cashel Blue, made in Tipperary; Bellingham Blue, made in County Louth; Abbey Blue, a Brie-style cheese made in County Laois; and Kerrygold, a major importer of commercially made fresh cheeses, recently introduced Kerrygold Blue. Blue cheese goes from starter to main course to cheese board so effortlessly that recipes hardly seem needed. Blue cheese–stuffed mushrooms like these are popular at many Irish pubs, such as Kyteler's Inn, in Kilkenny, where cream cheese and thyme are added, and at O'Shea's Merchant, in Dublin, where the chef serves them with a garlic and chive dip. I like these with marmalade-mustard sauce.

SERVES 4; MAKES ABOUT 1 CUP OF SAUCE

◆━━━━━━━━━ BLACKBOARD SPECIAL ━━━━━━━━━◆

BLUE CHEESE–STUFFED MUSHROOMS
with Marmalade-Mustard Sauce

◆━━━━━━━━━━━━━━━━━━━━━━━━━━◆

MARMALADE-MUSTARD SAUCE

1 cup orange marmalade

2 teaspoons English-style mustard, preferably Coleman's

2 teaspoons Irish whiskey

STUFFED MUSHROOMS

16 large white mushrooms, stems removed

8 ounces blue cheese, preferably Irish, at room temperature

3 ounces cream cheese, at room temperature

All-purpose flour for dredging

2 large eggs beaten with 2 tablespoons water

Fresh white bread crumbs for dredging (see Note, page 33)

Canola oil for frying

Mixed salad greens for garnish

1   **To make the sauce:** In a small saucepan over low heat, cook the marmalade for 2 to 3 minutes, or until slightly runny. Whisk in the mustard and whiskey. Transfer to 4 small ramekins or dishes and set aside.

2   **To make the stuffed mushrooms:** Wipe the mushroom caps with a moist paper towel. (Use the stems in a soup or omelet.) In a small bowl, combine the blue cheese and cream cheese. Mash with a fork until blended. With a small knife or spoon, stuff the mushroom caps with the cheese mixture. Put the flour in one shallow bowl, the egg wash in another, and the bread crumbs in a third. Dredge the mushrooms in the flour, dip in the egg wash, then cover with bread crumbs.

3   Pour 2 inches of oil into an electric skillet or a large stove-top pan and heat to 325°F. Drop the mushrooms, 2 at a time, into the hot oil. Cook, turning frequently with a wooden spoon, for 2 to 3 minutes, or until golden brown. With a slotted spoon, remove each mushroom as soon as it's browned, and drain on paper towels.

4   To serve, place the ramekins or dishes with the sauce in the center of 4 salad plates. Arrange some mixed greens around each ramekin and place 4 mushrooms on top.

CHAPTER 2

SOUPS

Ireland's climate is influenced by the warm waters of the Gulf Stream and the southwesterly winds coming in from the Atlantic Ocean. This makes for equitable conditions over the whole country and means Ireland is never exposed to extremes of weather. The coldest months are January and February, when the temperature might drop to as low as 34°F. But as residents know, it can rain at any time of the year and does so. When rain-laden winds blow in from the Atlantic and, as someone once described them, "damp the very marrow in your bones," it's soup that provides sustenance, warmth, and a big dose of comfort.

Soup, or "pottage" as it was once called, has been a staple in the diet of the Irish people for many centuries. According to the late food writer Theodora FitzGibbon, "Irish people will eat soup at every main meal both winter and summer." Whether it's a few vegetables tossed into a pot with some stock cubes, a simple broth created from long hours of stewing meat, or a coastal concoction of clams, mussels, or oysters, nothing says Irish food like soup, and it remains, without question, the most popular item on a pub menu. Brown soda bread (pages 95 and 98) comes along as a standard accompaniment.

Fitzpatrick's Pub and Restaurant in Rockmarshall, County Louth, is one of the most picturesque pubs in that part of the country, and possibly in all of Ireland. Located on the main Dundalk to Carlingford road, the pub is set against the leafy background of the Cooley Mountains, in the heart of the renowned Tain walking trail. Filled to the rafters with vintage signs, antiques, and kitchenware, Fitzpatrick's is consistently named a Black and White "Pub of the Year" award winner (see page 111) for its good food, charming atmosphere, and friendly service. Freshly caught seafood from nearby Carlingford is always featured, as in this popular seafood chowder, which I have adapted here. Serve this with brown soda bread (pages 95 and 98). **SERVES 4 TO 6**

SEAFOOD CHOWDER

½ cup (1 stick) plus 2 tablespoons unsalted Kerrygold Irish butter

½ cup all-purpose flour

4 cups milk, slightly warmed

2 leeks (white part only), washed and sliced

1 onion, chopped

1 carrot, peeled and grated

2 cups homemade fish stock (page 62), bottled clam juice, or 2 fish bouillon cubes mixed with 2 cups boiling water

¾ cup dry white wine

½ teaspoon minced garlic

¼ pound mussels, steamed, shells discarded

¼ pound clams, steamed, shells discarded

½ pound mixed seafood (such as salmon, shrimp, and scallops), cut into small pieces

Salt and freshly ground pepper to taste

1 tablespoon minced fresh herbs, such as basil, dill, chervil, and chives

1   In a medium saucepan over medium heat, melt $1/2$ cup of the butter. Stir in the flour and cook for 3 to 4 minutes, or until blended. Slowly whisk in the milk and cook, whisking constantly, for 3 to 5 minutes, or until the mixture is smooth. Set aside.

2   In a stockpot or large saucepan over medium heat, melt the remaining 2 tablespoons of butter. Add the leeks, onion, and carrot and cook, covered, stirring once or twice, for 5 to 7 minutes, or until the vegetables are soft but not browned. Add the fish stock or clam juice, wine, and garlic and cook, uncovered, for 5 to 7 minutes, or until the stock is reduced by half. Stir in the shellfish and seafood and cook for 5 to 7 minutes, or until the liquid is reduced again by half. Stir in the milk mixture, season with salt and pepper, and simmer until heated through.

3   To serve, ladle the chowder into shallow bowls and sprinkle with the mixed herbs.

· · · · ·

FITZPATRICK'S PUB, ROCKMARSHALL, COUNTY LOUTH

Vegetable soup, whether creamy like this one or with the vegetables left whole, is a staple of Irish home kitchens and pubs. At the Derg Inn, an acclaimed pub in the historic village of Terryglass, in County Tipperary, the chef uses as much Tipperary-grown produce as possible. Even the butter is produced by a local cooperative in nearby Nenagh. **SERVES 4 TO 6**

FARMHOUSE VEGETABLE SOUP

4 tablespoons unsalted Kerrygold Irish butter

1 small onion, chopped

2 leeks (white part only), washed and sliced

2 parsnips, peeled and sliced

2 medium potatoes, peeled and cut into 1-inch pieces

2 carrots, peeled and sliced

4 cups homemade vegetable stock (page 62), canned low-sodium vegetable broth, or 4 vegetable bouillon cubes mixed with 4 cups boiling water

⅔ cup half-and-half

3 tablespoons minced fresh flat-leaf parsley

Salt and freshly ground pepper to taste

1   In a stockpot or large saucepan over medium heat, melt the butter. Add the onion and leeks, cover, and cook, stirring once or twice, for 5 to 7 minutes, or until the vegetables are soft but not browned. Add the parsnips, potatoes, carrots, and stock or broth, cover, and cook for 25 to 30 minutes, or until the vegetables are tender. Remove from the heat and let cool for 10 minutes.

2   Working in batches, transfer the soup to a food processor or blender and purée until smooth. (Or purée in the pot with an immersion blender.) Return the soup to the pot, whisk in the half-and-half, and season with parsley, salt, and pepper. Simmer until heated through.

3   To serve, ladle the soup into shallow bowls.

• • • • •

THE CROWN BAR AND SALOON, BELFAST

Parsnips are one of Ireland's oldest vegetables and are often the basis for sweet dishes combined with fruit. This long, white vegetable is especially popular in winter, after the first frost of the year converts its starch to sugar and gives it a pleasant sweetness. It is a traditional ingredient in Irish soups. This recipe, a variation of which is found in many Irish pubs, contrasts the sweetness of parsnips with the tartness of Granny Smith apples. Serve it topped with Blue Cheese Toasts, if desired, or homemade croutons (page 78). **SERVES 4 TO 6**

PARSNIP AND APPLE SOUP

6 tablespoons unsalted Kerrygold Irish butter

1 medium onion, chopped

5 parsnips, peeled and chopped

3 Granny Smith apples, peeled, cored, and chopped

1 medium potato, peeled and cut into 1-inch pieces

6 cups homemade vegetable stock (page 62), canned low-sodium vegetable broth, or 6 vegetable bouillon cubes mixed with 6 cups boiling water

2 teaspoons curry powder

1 teaspoon ground cumin

1 teaspoon ground coriander

Salt and freshly ground pepper to taste

½ cup half-and-half

Minced fresh chives for garnish

Blue Cheese Toasts (optional, facing page)

1   In a stockpot or large saucepan over medium heat, melt the butter. Add the onion and cook for 3 to 5 minutes, or until soft but not browned. Add the parsnips, apples, and potato and stir well to coat. Cover the pan, reduce the heat, and cook the vegetables, stirring once or twice, for 10 to 12 minutes, or until the apples begin to break up. Uncover, add the stock or broth, curry powder, cumin, coriander, salt, and pepper, and bring to a boil. Re-cover, reduce the heat to low, and simmer for 35 to 40 minutes, or until the vegetables are tender. Remove from the heat and let cool for 10 minutes.

2   Working in batches, transfer the soup to a food processor or blender and purée until smooth. (Or purée in the pot with an immersion blender.) Return the soup to the pot, whisk in the half-and-half, and adjust the seasoning. Simmer until heated through.

3   To serve, ladle the soup into shallow bowls, sprinkle with chives, and top with 2 Blue Cheese Toasts, if desired.

Blue Cheese Toasts   MAKES 8 TO 10 TOASTS

1 baguette or another type of French bread   ½ cup blue cheese, preferably Irish
⅓ cup plus 2 teaspoons extra virgin olive oil

1   Preheat the broiler. Cut eight to ten ½-inch-thick slices from a baguette.

2   Toast the slices on a rack under the broiler about 4 inches from the heat, turning them once, or until lightly toasted. Remove from the broiler and brush the slices on each side with the ⅓ cup of olive oil.

3   In a small bowl, mash the blue cheese with the remaining 2 teaspoons of olive oil. Spread the mixture evenly over one side of each slice of toast. Broil the toasts on a baking sheet for 1 minute, or until the cheese is melted and lightly browned. Remove from the oven and let cool on a wire rack.

Hillsborough, in County Down, is an unspoiled village full of eighteenth-century Georgian buildings, including Hillsborough Castle (built in 1779), the courthouse (built in 1760), and the Plough Inn, a former coaching inn owned by chef Derek Patterson, who has been wowing patrons at his premises on the village square since 1984. The Plough Inn is actually three separate entities—a pub, restaurant, and more recently, a café-bar-grill, each with its own style of cuisine. In the pub, Patterson sweetens an autumnal pumpkin soup with a whole vanilla bean, then balances its rich flavor with lusty wild garlic. For maximum flavor, slice the bean, which is actually a seedpod, down its length, and scrape the point of the knife along the inside to release the tiny seeds. Serve this with brown soda bread (pages 95 and 98). **SERVES 4 TO 6**

Pumpkin, Vanilla, and
WILD-GARLIC SOUP

1 vanilla bean

6 tablespoons unsalted Kerrygold Irish butter

1 clove garlic, minced

2 onions, chopped

2 pounds pumpkin, or Hubbard or butternut squash, peeled, seeded, and chopped into 1-inch pieces

2 cups homemade chicken stock (page 60), canned low-sodium chicken broth, or 2 chicken bouillon cubes mixed with 2 cups boiling water

2 cups half-and-half

Sea salt and freshly ground pepper to taste

6 tablespoons crème fraîche (see Note)

1   Split the vanilla bean pod, remove the seeds, and set the pod and seeds aside. In a stockpot or large saucepan over medium heat, melt the butter. Add the garlic and onions and cook for 3 to 5 minutes, or until soft but not browned. Add the pumpkin, chicken stock or broth, and vanilla bean pod (but not the seeds), and cook, covered, for 20 to 25 minutes, or until the pumpkin is tender. Remove from the heat and let cool for 10 minutes. Remove the pod.

2   Working in batches, transfer the soup to a food processor or blender and purée until smooth. (Or purée in the pot with an immersion blender.) Return the soup to the pot, whisk in the half-and-half, and season with salt and pepper. Stir in the vanilla seeds, and simmer until heated through.

3   To serve, ladle the soup into shallow bowls and swirl a tablespoon of crème fraîche into each one.

NOTE: *To make crème fraîche, combine 1 cup of heavy (whipping) cream with 1 tablespoon of buttermilk in a glass jar. Stir to blend, then cover and let stand at room temperature for 12 to 24 hours, or until thickened. Refrigerate until ready to use.*

The test kitchen of Bord Bia, the Irish Food Board, is a great source of recipes that feature the country's world-class dairy products and fresh produce, like this combination of hearty cauliflower, potatoes, celery, and cream. A version of this recipe will be found on the menu of many pubs in Ireland. Serve it with Cheddar-Walnut Bread (page 72), a pleasant alternative to traditional brown soda bread. **SERVES 4 TO 6**

CREAM OF CAULIFLOWER SOUP

2 tablespoons unsalted Kerrygold Irish butter

1 tablespoon olive oil

2 leeks (white part only), washed and sliced

1 small onion, chopped

2 celery stalks, chopped

1 tablespoon minced fresh thyme

1 large head cauliflower, cut into florets

4 cups homemade chicken stock (page 60), canned low-sodium chicken broth, or 4 chicken bouillon cubes mixed with 4 cups boiling water

1 cup half-and-half

Salt and freshly ground pepper to taste

Pinch of cayenne pepper

Pinch of curry powder (optional)

Minced fresh chives for garnish

1   In a stockpot or large saucepan over medium heat, melt the butter with the olive oil. Add the leeks, onion, celery, and thyme and cook for 8 to 10 minutes, or until the vegetables are soft but not browned. Add the cauliflower and cook for 8 to 10 minutes, or until slightly soft. Add the stock or broth, bring to a boil, then reduce the heat to low. Simmer, covered, for 15 to 18 minutes, or until the cauliflower is tender. Remove from the heat and let cool for 10 minutes.

2   Working in batches, transfer the soup to a food processor or blender and purée until smooth. (Or purée in the pot with an immersion blender.) Return the soup to the pot, whisk in the half-and-half, and season with salt, pepper, cayenne, and curry, if using. Simmer until heated through.

3   To serve, ladle the soup into shallow bowls and sprinkle with chives.

SOUP AND A SANDWICH

Nothing says "pub grub" more than the long-standing combination of soup and a sandwich. My first introduction to Irish food was a toasted cheese sandwich at a seaside pub in Lahinch, County Clare. To be honest, back in 1984 there was little choice about what to order in a pub—it was a sandwich along with a bag of crisps, or nothing at all! Since most pubs started out in the "wet trade," which meant they only sold drinks, the transition to serving food was most easily accomplished by putting on a pot of soup and offering it with either slices of brown soda bread or some type of meat or cheese tucked between pieces of "store-bought" white bread.

The first sandwich was made for John Montague (1718–1792), the Fourth Earl of Sandwich. Montague was a hardened gambler who sometimes refused to get up from the gambling table even for meals. History tells us that during one furious game, when he couldn't afford a break, he ordered his valet to bring him meat wedged between two pieces of bread. Others soon began to order "the same as Sandwich," in reference to his title. That first sandwich happened to be a piece of salt beef tucked between two slices of toasted bread.

Fortunately, the contents of a sandwich and the state of affairs in an Irish pub kitchen have both vastly improved, and the sandwich is as popular as ever. Fillings range from farmhouse cheese to roast peppered beef or prawn salad. Nowadays, the bread might be a baguette, a sandwich roll called a "bap," rye bread, or a tortilla wrap. Garlic-flavored or spicy mayonnaise, tomato or crab apple chutney, pineapple or tomato salsa, and raisin or onion relish are likely spreads.

Paddy Burkes Oyster Inn in Clarenbridge, County Galway, is renowned for its seafood—especially oysters—and for its involvement with the Clarenbridge Oyster Festival each September (see page 17). There the chef also uses locally grown seasonal produce for his soup of the day, like this colorful one made with red, yellow, and orange peppers. He tempers the bite of the peppers with smooth crème fraîche, which he swirls in just before serving. Accompany this with brown soda bread (pages 95 and 98). **SERVES 4 TO 6**

PADDY BURKES PEPPER SOUP

½ cup (1 stick) unsalted Kerrygold Irish butter

4 bell peppers (a combination of red, yellow, and orange), seeded, deribbed, and diced

1 red onion, chopped

1 cup all-purpose flour

6 cups homemade vegetable stock (page 62), canned low-sodium vegetable broth, or 6 vegetable bouillon cubes mixed with 6 cups boiling water

⅔ cup half-and-half

1 tablespoon minced fresh basil

1 tablespoon minced fresh flat-leaf parsley

Salt and freshly ground pepper to taste

6 tablespoons crème fraîche (see Note, page 46)

1 In a stockpot or large saucepan over medium heat, melt the butter. Add the peppers and onion and cook, covered, stirring once or twice, for 5 to 7 minutes, or until the vegetables are tender but not browned. Stir in the flour until blended with the vegetables. Add the stock or broth, a cup at a time, stirring after each addition to blend with the flour and vegetables. Reduce the heat to low and simmer for 50 to 60 minutes, or until the vegetables are tender. Remove from the heat and let cool for 10 minutes.

CONTINUED

2   Working in batches, transfer the mixture to a food processor or blender and purée until smooth. (Or purée in the pot with an immersion blender.) Return the soup to the pot, whisk in the half-and-half, and season with the basil, parsley, salt, and pepper. Simmer until heated through.

3   To serve, ladle the soup into shallow bowls and swirl a tablespoon of crème fraîche into each one.

VARIATION:

Cream of Chicken and Pepper Soup

At the Garrick Bar on Chichester Street in Belfast, the chef makes a similar pepper soup but adds chicken and cream. Follow the recipe as described above, adding 2 boneless chicken breasts, cut into $1/2$-inch pieces, to the soup after the stock has been added. Simmer for 1 hour, then let cool for 10 minutes. Continue with the recipe, substituting light cream for the half-and-half and omitting the basil and crème fraîche.

TRADITIONAL IRISH BACON

All bacon is not created equal, so when it comes to using bacon for the recipes in this book, you have to think outside the box—or in this case, outside the package of conventional sliced breakfast bacon. Here's why:

For many years, the most important meat in Ireland was pork, either fresh, or cured as bacon, and even today the popularity of pork and pork products is unwavering. In Ireland, only the leg of the pig is called "ham" (it's also called "gammon"); otherwise, the cured meat is bacon.

Back bacon, from which rashers come, is actually cut from the loin and cured in spices. It can be cooked as a joint or roast (often glazed with a sweet red currant or tangy mustard sauce), cut into chops, or added to dishes like Roast Chicken with Bacon and Leeks (page 131). Streaky rashers, which are the most flavorful cut because they have a bit more fat, are fried crisp at breakfast, used in sandwiches and soups, in salads such as Bibb, Bacon, and Apple Salad (page 77), and in seafood dishes like Roasted Monkfish Wrapped in Bacon (page 158). The shoulder or collar of bacon (also called "boiling bacon") is the traditional cut for Bacon and Cabbage (page 125), but it is also ideal for a wide range of other dishes. Cut into chunks, it adds flavor to casseroles like Dublin Coddle (page 100), bean dishes, and pasta dishes. To find traditional Irish bacon, see Resources, page 214.

My mother used to make a traditional split pea soup with dried split peas and a leftover ham bone, but I always found it too thick and heavy. On a recent visit to County Fermanagh, I tasted this much lighter soup made with fresh peas, which makes a refreshing change from the classic. There it was topped with homemade croutons (page 78), but it's also delightful with shavings of aged Gabriel cheese, a hard cheese similar to Parmesan, produced by the West Cork Natural Cheese Company in Schull, County Cork. **SERVES 4 TO 6**

SPRING PEA SOUP

2 tablespoons unsalted Kerrygold Irish butter

1 medium onion, chopped

4 packages ham-flavored bouillon, such as Goya or Knorr brand, mixed with 4 cups boiling water

1 medium potato, peeled and cut into ½-inch pieces

1 pound fresh peas, shelled, or frozen petite peas

1 cup half-and-half

Salt and freshly ground pepper to taste

Homemade croutons (page 78)

1   In a stockpot or large saucepan over medium heat, melt the butter. Stir in the onion and cook for 3 to 5 minutes, or until soft but not browned. Add the bouillon and bring to a boil. Add the potato, reduce the heat to low, and simmer for 10 to 12 minutes, or until the potato is tender. Add the peas (if using frozen, return to a boil for a moment), and simmer for 5 to 7 minutes, or until tender. Remove from the heat and let cool for 10 minutes.

2   Working in batches, transfer the mixture to a food processor or blender and purée until smooth. (Or purée in the pot with an immersion blender.) Return the soup to the pot, whisk in the half-and-half, and simmer until heated through. Season with salt and pepper.

3   To serve, ladle the soup into shallow bowls and sprinkle with some croutons.

Moone High Cross Inn at Bolton Hill, in Moone, County Kildare, is a rambling eighteenth-century country inn operated by the Clinchy family. It makes an ideal stop along the N-9 route between Dublin and Kilkenny. In addition to the picturesque location, original interior, and quirky, bric-a-brac-filled courtyard, there's always traditional home cooking and convivial conversation on the pub's menu, which explains why it was named County Kildare "Pub of the Year" in the 2004 Black and White pub awards competition (see page 111). The fact that it's been a favorite watering hole for celebrities such as Clint Eastwood adds to its charm. This traditional potato and leek soup is always "on the hob."
SERVES 6 TO 8

POTATO-LEEK SOUP

2 tablespoons unsalted Kerrygold Irish butter

3 leeks (white part only), washed and sliced

1 large onion, chopped

6 medium potatoes, peeled and cut into
   1-inch pieces

6 cups homemade vegetable stock (page 62),
   canned low-sodium vegetable broth, or
6 vegetable bouillon cubes mixed with
   6 cups boiling water

1¼ cups half-and-half

Salt and freshly ground pepper to taste

Minced fresh flat-leaf parsley for garnish

1   In a stockpot or large saucepan over medium heat, melt the butter. Add the leeks and onion, cover, and cook, stirring once or twice, for 5 to 7 minutes, or until the vegetables are soft but not browned. Add the potatoes and stock or broth, cover, and cook for 35 to 40 minutes, or until the vegetables are tender. Remove from the heat and let cool for 10 minutes.

2   Working in batches, transfer the soup to a food processor or blender and purée until smooth. (Or purée in the pot with an immersion blender.) Return the soup to the pot, whisk in the half-and-half, and season with salt and pepper. Simmer until heated through.

3   To serve, ladle the soup into shallow bowls and sprinkle with parsley.

• • • • •

FOLLOWING PAGES: MOONE HIGH CROSS INN, MOONE, COUNTY KILDARE

H CROSS INN
Quality Wines Beers, Spirits & Tobaccos
EGON
RONAY'S
GUIDES

Bord Bia, the Irish Food Board, provides resources, recipes, and advice to consumers and chefs alike on all aspects of Irish food and drink. They devised this recipe to utilize three Irish staples—bacon, potatoes, and blue cheese—then added zucchini, which the Irish call "courgettes," for additional flavor and color. The soup frequently appears as a blackboard special in Irish pubs. **SERVES 4 TO 6**

BLACKBOARD SPECIAL

Bacon, Blue Cheese, and
COURGETTE SOUP

2 tablespoons olive oil

5 to 6 streaky rashers (traditional Irish bacon; see page 53), diced

1 medium onion, chopped

3 medium zucchini, sliced, and a few slices reserved for garnish

3 medium potatoes, peeled and cut into ½-inch pieces

4 cups homemade chicken stock (page 60), canned low-sodium chicken broth, or 4 chicken bouillon cubes mixed with 4 cups boiling water

4 ounces blue cheese, preferably Irish, crumbled

⅔ cup half-and-half

Freshly ground pepper to taste

3 tablespoons minced fresh flat-leaf parsley

1   In a stockpot or large saucepan over medium heat, warm the oil. Add the bacon and cook for 2 to 3 minutes, or until nearly crisp. With a slotted spoon, remove a few pieces and reserve for a garnish. Stir in the onion, zucchini, and potatoes. Cover and cook, stirring once or twice, for 5 to 7 minutes, or until the onion and zucchini are soft but not browned. Stir in the stock or broth and bring to a boil. Lower the heat and simmer, covered, for 12 to 15 minutes, or until the potatoes are tender. Remove from the heat and let cool for 10 minutes.

2   Working in batches, transfer the soup to a food processor or blender and purée until smooth. (Or purée in the pot with an immersion blender.) Return the soup to the pot, whisk in the cheese and half-and-half, and season with pepper. Simmer until heated through.

3   To serve, ladle the soup into shallow bowls and garnish with the reserved bacon and zucchini slices, and the parsley.

HOMEMADE STOCKS

Chicken Stock MAKES ABOUT 5 CUPS

1½ pounds chicken pieces (a combination of backs, wings, and necks) and bones

6 cups cold water

1 onion, chopped

1 leek (white part only), washed and chopped

1 carrot, peeled and chopped

1 celery stalk, chopped

1 teaspoon salt

1 teaspoon black peppercorns

1 bouquet garni (a cheesecloth bag containing 3 sprigs fresh flat-leaf parsley, 1 sprig fresh thyme, and 1 bay leaf)

In a large stockpot or Dutch oven over medium heat, combine the chicken pieces and bones and water. Bring to a boil and skim any foam that rises to the top. Reduce the heat to medium-low, skim again, and add the onion, leek, carrot, celery, salt, peppercorns, and bouquet garni. Simmer, skimming occasionally, for 2 to 2½ hours. Strain the stock through a fine-mesh sieve into a bowl and let cool. Refrigerate for several hours, remove the congealed fat, then cover and refrigerate for up to 1 week or freeze for up to 3 months.

Beef Stock MAKES ABOUT 8 CUPS

4 pounds beef shanks or short ribs	2 celery stalks
2 onions, quartered	1½ tcaspoons salt
1 carrot, peeled and quartered	1 bouquet garni (a cheesecloth bag containing
4 quarts cold water	3 sprigs fresh flat-leaf parsley, 1 sprig fresh
	thyme, and 1 bay leaf)

1 Put the oven rack in the middle position, and preheat the oven to 450°F.

2 In a large roasting pan or ovenproof casserole, combine the beef shanks or ribs, onions, and carrot. Roast, turning 2 to 3 times, for about 1 hour, or until the bones and vegetables are browned.

3 Transfer the meat and vegetables to a large stockpot or Dutch oven. Add 2 cups of the water to the roasting pan and deglaze by boiling over high heat and stirring and scraping up the browned bits with a wooden spoon for 1 minute. Add the deglazing liquid to the stockpot along with the remaining water, the celery, salt, and bouquet garni. Bring to a boil, and skim any foam that rises to the top. Reduce the heat to medium-low and simmer, uncovered, for 1 to 1 ½ hours.

4 Strain the stock through a fine-mesh sieve into a bowl and let cool. Refrigerate for several hours, remove the congealed fat, then cover and refrigerate for up to 1 week or freeze for up to 3 months.

Fish Stock MAKES ABOUT 3 CUPS

1 pound bones and trimmings of any
   white-fleshed fish
1 large onion, sliced
12 sprigs fresh flat-leaf parsley

2 tablespoons fresh lemon juice
½ teaspoon salt
3½ cups cold water
½ cup dry white wine

In a large stockpot or Dutch oven over medium heat, combine the bones and trimmings, the onion, parsley, lemon juice, and salt. Cover and cook for 5 minutes. Add the water and wine. Bring to a boil, skim any foam that rises to the top, then reduce the heat to low and simmer for 20 minutes. Strain the stock through a fine-mesh sieve into a bowl and let cool. Cover and refrigerate for up to 3 days or freeze for up to 3 months.

Vegetable Stock MAKES ABOUT 4 CUPS

1½ tablespoons unsalted Kerrygold Irish butter
2 onions, peeled and chopped
1 leek (white part only), washed and chopped
1 carrot, peeled and chopped
1 celery stalk, chopped
5 large white mushrooms, chopped
1 potato, peeled and cut into ½-inch pieces

6⅓ cups cold water
3 garlic cloves, peeled and minced
1 teaspoon black peppercorns
¼ teaspoon dried thyme
½ bay leaf
6 sprigs fresh flat-leaf parsley
½ teaspoon salt

In a stockpot or large saucepan over medium heat, melt the butter. Add the onions and cook for 5 minutes, or until lightly browned. Add the leek, carrot, celery, mushrooms, potato, and ⅓ cup of the water. Cook, covered, for 5 minutes, or until the vegetables are slightly tender. Add the remaining 6 cups of water, the garlic, peppercorns, thyme, bay leaf, parsley, and salt. Bring to a boil, reduce the heat to low, and simmer, uncovered, for 2 hours. Strain the stock through a fine-mesh sieve into a bowl and let cool. Cover and refrigerate for up to 1 week or freeze for up to 3 months.

• • • • •
NOLAN'S, ROSSCARBERRY, COUNTY CORK

CHAPTER 3

SALADS

For many years, a side salad (a slice or two of tomato and cucumber atop a few leaves of lettuce) was really just a garnish for a main course in most Irish pubs and restaurants. Today main-dish salads of mixed greens topped with deep-fried cheese, smoked chicken, and pan-fried scallops are as commonplace as Irish stew. Most cooks would prefer to buy individual heads of lettuce, but for variety and convenience, packages labeled "spring mix," "mâche," "mesclun," or "field greens" are a suitable alternative. Packaged greens can include any combination of the following lettuces: crisphead (iceberg), butterhead (Boston or Bibb), leaf (oak leaf, frilly red leaf, crinkly green leaf), romaine (also called "Cos lettuce"), and frisée (a member of the chicory family). Other ingredients you'll find in pub salads are baby spinach, peppery arugula (also known as "rocket" in Ireland), Belgian endive, curly endive, and radicchio (a red-leafed Italian chicory). Three ounces ($1^{1}/_{2}$ to 2 cups) of loosely packed leaves is the recommended serving size.

•••••

THE PLOUGH INN, HILLSBOROUGH, COUNTY DOWN

Chef Derek Patterson has owned the Plough Inn, a former coaching inn in the lovely County Down village of Hillsborough, for two decades. Known for his innovative style, Patterson operates three rather distinct restaurants at his premises on the Square—a pub, restaurant, and café-bar-grill. This crunchy, Asian-inspired salad with a lively dressing is served in the pub. **SERVES 4**

CHICKEN AND ROASTED ASPARAGUS SALAD
with Ginger-Sesame Dressing

GINGER-SESAME DRESSING

⅓ cup toasted sesame oil

⅓ cup light soy sauce

3 tablespoons fresh lime juice

1 tablespoon minced fresh ginger

1 tablespoon minced garlic

1 bunch asparagus, tough ends snapped off

2 tablespoons olive oil

Salt and freshly ground pepper to taste

6 ounces sugar snap peas, strings removed (see Note)

½ cup water

Two 6-ounce boneless, skinless chicken breast halves

1 large bunch rocket (arugula) or watercress

1 cup bean sprouts

½ jalapeño pepper, thinly sliced (optional)

1 teaspoon sesame seeds, toasted

1. **To make the dressing:** Combine all the ingredients in a lidded jar, cover, and shake until blended. Set aside.

2. Prepare a medium-hot fire in a charcoal grill or preheat a gas grill to medium-high. Preheat the oven to 450°F.

3. **To start the salad:** Arrange the asparagus in a single layer on a large baking sheet. Drizzle with the oil and season with salt and pepper. Turn the asparagus to coat. Roast, turning occasionally, for 10 to 12 minutes, or until crisp-tender. Set aside and let cool. In a small saucepan, bring the sugar snap peas and water to a boil. Cook for 2 to 3 minutes, or until the snap peas are crisp-tender. Drain and rinse in cold water.

4. Season the chicken with salt and pepper and grill for 5 to 7 minutes on each side, or until no longer pink in the center. Cut into thin strips.

5. **To compose the salads:** In a large bowl, toss the rocket (arugula) or watercress, asparagus, and sugar snap peas with the dressing. Divide the greens among 4 salad plates. Top with the warm chicken, bean sprouts, jalapeño pepper, if using, and the sesame seeds.

NOTE: *Sugar snap peas are a sweet, crunchy cross between English peas and snow peas. They have strings on both seams that should be removed before eating. Just snap off a bit of the stem and pull gently down both sides. Sugar snaps should be cooked very briefly to retain their color, crispness, and flavor.*

One of the most popular locations in the Shannon region is the village of Bunratty, County Clare, where Bunratty Castle, Bunratty Folk Park, Bunratty Winery, and Durty Nelly's pub-restaurant play a prominent role in the area's tourist industry. Also known as the Village Inn, Durty Nelly's was established in 1620. Because of its location just feet away from the castle, it likes to boast that it "nestles in the shadow of history." The original Durty Nelly was the keeper of the toll bridge over the river Owengarney, which flows alongside the pub on its way to join the Shannon, and her history is indeed a lively one (see page 86). Today the building consists of what's called a local bar (popular year-round with patrons who live and work in the area), with an open fire and old stone floor strewn with timber shavings; an upstairs bar; a main bar; and two restaurants, which serve lunch and dinner. When the weather cooperates, there's outdoor seating in front of the castle, where you can order this summery salad tossed with a rich walnut vinaigrette. Serve it with Cheddar-Walnut Bread (recipe follows), an interesting variation on traditional brown soda bread. **SERVES 4**

SMOKED CHICKEN AND AVOCADO SALAD
with Walnut Vinaigrette

WALNUT VINAIGRETTE
⅓ cup walnut oil
2 tablespoons white wine vinegar
Salt and freshly ground pepper to taste

5 ounces mixed salad greens
Two 6-ounce smoked chicken breast halves, sliced and shredded (see Note)
1 avocado, peeled, pitted, and sliced
Minced fresh herbs, such as dill, coriander, and parsley, for garnish
Cheddar-Walnut Bread for serving (optional, page 72)

CONTINUED

•••••
DURTY NELLY'S, BUNRATTY, COUNTY CLARE

1 **To make the vinaigrette:** Combine all the ingredients in a lidded jar, cover, and shake until blended.

2 **To compose the salads:** In a large bowl, toss the mixed greens with the vinaigrette. Divide the greens among 4 salad plates. Arrange the chicken and avocado on top. Garnish with the fresh herbs and accompany with the cheddar-walnut bread, if desired.

NOTE: *Smoked chicken breasts can be found at specialty butchers and delicatessens. Or you can smoke chicken yourself with a stove-top smoker, such as Cameron's brand (see Resources, page 214).*

Cheddar-Walnut Bread   MAKES 1 LOAF

1½ cups self-rising flour
½ cup whole wheat flour
1 teaspoon dry mustard
¼ teaspoon salt
½ teaspoon baking powder
½ teaspoon baking soda
2 teaspoons sugar

6 tablespoons unsalted Kerrygold Irish butter, cut into small pieces
5 ounces Kerrygold Vintage Cheddar cheese, grated (about 1¼ cups)
½ cup walnuts, chopped
2 large eggs
1 cup buttermilk

1 Preheat the oven to 375°F. Lightly butter a 9-by-5-by-3-inch loaf pan.

2 In a food processor, combine the flours, mustard, salt, baking powder, baking soda, and sugar. Pulse 2 to 3 times to blend. Add the butter and process for 10 to 15 seconds, or until the mixture resembles coarse crumbs. Set aside 1 tablespoon of the cheese and 1 tablespoon of the walnuts for the topping, and add the rest to the food processor, pulsing 8 to 10 times to blend.

3 Add the eggs and buttermilk and process for 10 to 20 seconds, or until a soft dough forms. Spoon into the prepared pan, smooth the top with a rubber spatula that has been dipped in buttermilk, and sprinkle the remaining cheese and walnuts over the top.

4 Bake for 35 to 40 minutes, or until a skewer inserted into the center comes out clean. Remove from the oven and let cool on a wire rack before slicing.

Located in Crinkill, just outside the heritage town of Birr, in County Offaly, the Thatch Bar and Restaurant is exactly what you'd expect an Irish pub to look like, both inside and out. The thatched building has been licensed for over 250 years and consists of a series of interconnecting rooms that share two fireplaces. Old pine furniture and antique china complete the look. The real draw here, though, is the food—expect anything from wild boar and ostrich to caviar and escargots. Many feel the kitchen is among the most innovative in the Midlands. This hearty salad gets a kick from jalapeño pepper and color from the red leaf lettuce and radicchio. Serve it with brown soda bread (pages 95 and 98). **SERVES 4**

CRAB AND AVOCADO TIAN

¾ pound fresh crabmeat

¼ cup minced fresh chives

3 tablespoons minced jalapeño pepper

¼ cup mayonnaise

Salt and freshly ground pepper to taste

2 ripe avocados, peeled and pitted

¼ cup fresh lemon juice

Pepper-flavored oil for drizzling

4 ounces red leaf lettuce

1 small head radicchio, chopped

Lemon wedges for garnish

1   In a medium bowl, combine the crabmeat, chives, 1 tablespoon of the jalapeño, the mayonnaise, salt, and pepper. In another medium bowl, mash the avocados. Stir in the lemon juice and remaining 2 tablespoons of the jalapeño.

2   **To compose the salads:** Lightly oil a 3-inch pastry cutter with pepper-flavored oil and place in the center of a salad plate. Spread a quarter of the crabmeat mixture into the ring and press down firmly with the back of a spoon to help the mixture hold its shape. Spread a quarter of the avocado mixture over the top. Gently lift the ring. Repeat 3 more times with the remaining crabmeat and avocado mixtures. Refrigerate the plates for 30 minutes. Arrange the red leaf lettuce and radicchio around the crabmeat molds. Garnish each serving with a wedge of lemon, and drizzle the pepper-flavored oil over the lettuce and radicchio.

Situated in the idyllic Vale of Avoca in County Wicklow, the Meetings is a perfect spot for lunch or dinner, a cup of coffee or tea, or traditional Irish music. Named for the junction where the Avonmore and Avonbeag Rivers meet, the pub hosts entertainment every night during the summer months and a traditional *ceili* (Irish music and dance) on Sunday afternoons. Lovers of Irish poetry will enjoy a visit, too, as the place also served as inspiration for Ireland's national poet, Thomas Moore, who immortalized the area in his poem "The Meeting of the Waters." The food is wholesome and hearty, but with a twenty-first-century touch, thanks to chef Dermot Moore, whose parents own the premises. In this unusual chicken salad, the "pancake" is a batter-fried chicken breast. Serve it with Blue Cheese Toasts (page 45), if you wish. The Meetings is a member of Irish Pubs of Distinction (see page 159). **SERVES 4**

PANCAKE CHICKEN SALAD
with Raspberry-Mustard Vinaigrette

RASPBERRY-MUSTARD VINAIGRETTE

2 tablespoons Dijon mustard

3 tablespoons raspberry vinegar

6 tablespoons extra virgin olive oil

Freshly ground pepper to taste

PANCAKE CHICKEN

2 large eggs

½ cup milk

1 tablespoon minced garlic

¼ teaspoon ground turmeric

¼ teaspoon ground coriander

¼ teaspoon ground ginger

1 cup self-rising flour

Canola oil for frying

Four 6-ounce boneless, skinless chicken breast halves, cut into 2 to 3 strips each

3 ounces mixed romaine lettuce and rocket (arugula)

2 ounces red leaf lettuce

¼ cup dried cranberries

1. **To make the vinaigrette:** Combine all the ingredients in a lidded jar, cover, and shake to blend. Set aside.

2. **To make the chicken:** In a medium bowl, whisk together the eggs and milk. Stir in the garlic and spices. Whisk in the flour, a tablespoonful at a time, and continue to whisk until the batter is smooth. Let rest for 5 minutes.

3. Preheat the oven to 400°F. Lightly grease a baking pan large enough to hold the chicken in one layer.

4. In a large skillet over medium heat, heat 2 inches of oil until very hot. (To test, drop a small spoonful of batter into the oil. When it's brown and crisp, the oil is hot enough.) Dredge the chicken breasts in the batter and cook for 1 to 2 minutes on each side, or until lightly browned. With tongs, remove the chicken from the skillet and transfer it to the prepared pan. Bake for 20 to 22 minutes, or until the chicken is no longer pink inside.

5. **To compose the salads:** In a large bowl, toss the greens with the vinaigrette. Divide the greens among 4 salad plates and place the chicken pieces on top of each serving. Sprinkle the cranberries around the chicken.

Delicate Bibb lettuce (also known as butterhead lettuce), crisp Irish bacon, and chopped apple are the basis for this salad, devised by Bord Bia, the Irish Food Board, to showcase Irish products. It's topped with a creamy salad dressing made with a Camembert-style cheese. Several Irish cheese makers produce Camembert. Cooleeney and Carrigbyrne Farmhouse's St. Killian are both fine examples. These rich and creamy cow's milk cheeses with a white rind and smooth interior are ideal for this salad.
SERVES 4

BIBB, BACON, AND APPLE SALAD
with Camembert Dressing

CAMEMBERT DRESSING

⅔ cup sour cream

1 tablespoon apple cider

2 ounces Camembert-style cheese, preferably Irish, rind removed and chopped

Dash of cider vinegar

4 streaky rashers (traditional Irish bacon; see page 53)

3 tablespoons olive oil

1 Granny Smith apple, cored and chopped

Salt and freshly ground pepper to taste

2 small heads of Bibb or Boston lettuce, torn into pieces

1 tablespoon fresh lemon juice

1   **To make the dressing:** In a small saucepan over medium-low heat, whisk together the sour cream, cider, cheese, and vinegar. Cook for 3 to 5 minutes, or until the cheese has melted and the mixture is smooth and creamy. Set aside.

2   In a large skillet, cook the bacon over medium heat for 5 to 7 minutes, or until crisp. With a slotted spoon, remove the bacon from the skillet and transfer to paper towels to drain. When cool, finely chop the bacon. Return the skillet to medium heat, add 1 tablespoon of the olive oil and the apples. Sauté the apples for 3 to 5 minutes, or until slightly tender. Season with salt and pepper.

3   **To compose the salads:** Divide the lettuce among 4 salad plates. Drizzle with the remaining 2 tablespoons of olive oil and the lemon juice. Top the lettuce with the warm apples and bacon, and spoon the dressing over all.

A ploughman's lunch is a traditional salad that is usually made with sliced meat—most often chicken, turkey, ham, or roast beef—and always with a slice of Cheddar cheese. Popular in the United Kingdom as well as in Ireland, the salad is open to wide interpretation. It is generally accompanied by a serving of coleslaw or chutney or a few slices of tomato, cucumber, apple, or pear. A ploughman's lunch is generally served in Irish pubs with a basket of brown soda bread (pages 95 and 98) or crusty French bread. In Kenmare, County Kerry, a town often referred to as "the jewel in the Ring of Kerry," O'Donnábhain's Pub on Henry Street serves its ploughman's lunch with home-cooked honey-and-mustard-baked ham and a ramekin filled with the chef's homemade Tomato Chutney. **SERVES 4**

PLOUGHMAN'S LUNCH

3 ounces mixed salad greens

Whole-grain mustard vinaigrette (page 84)

8 to 12 slices honey-baked ham, cut into triangles

8 to 12 slices of Kerrygold Vintage Cheddar cheese, cut into triangles

1 tomato, cut into wedges

½ red onion, grated

1 carrot, peeled and julienned

1 cucumber, sliced

8 to 10 black olives

Tomato Chutney for serving (page 82)

Brown soda bread (pages 95 and 98) or French bread for serving

⅂ **To compose the salads:** Divide the mixed greens among 4 salad plates. Drizzle with the vinaigrette. Arrange the slices of meat and cheese over the greens and garnish with the tomato wedges, red onion, carrot, cucumber, and olives. Spoon the chutney into a ramekin and serve with the salad and slices of bread.

CONTINUED

Tomato Chutney   MAKES ABOUT 2 CUPS

1 cup sugar

1½ cups cider vinegar

2 teaspoons sea salt

1 teaspoon crushed cardamom seeds

1 teaspoon ground ginger

½ teaspoon mustard seeds

¼ teaspoon ground cloves

1½ pounds plum tomatoes, quartered

1 medium onion, chopped

2 tablespoons minced garlic

1 tablespoon olive oil

½ cup golden raisins

Freshly ground pepper to taste

In a large saucepan over medium-low heat, combine the sugar, vinegar, salt, cardamom, ginger, mustard seeds, and cloves. Slowly bring the mixture to a boil, stirring until the sugar is dissolved. Add the tomatoes, onion, garlic, olive oil, raisins, and pepper. Reduce the heat to low, and simmer, uncovered, stirring frequently, for 1 to 1¼ hours, or until the mixture is thickened. (After a few minutes' cooking time, the tomato skins will separate from the pulp. Remove the skins with a fork and discard.) Spoon the chutney into a clean jar or bowl, cover, and refrigerate for up to 3 weeks.

THE IRISH PUB COMPANY

There's nothing in the world quite like an Irish pub, a rare mix of music, conversation, food, drink, hospitality, and humor. If you're interested in starting a business, you can add "exceptional investment opportunity" to the list as well. The Irish have always recognized the appeal of the atmosphere and attractive sociability of a pub, and now other nationalities have come to the same conclusion. From Dublin to Dubai and Roscommon to Rome, a new generation of Irish pubs has developed from a concept into a phenomenon under the guidance of Guinness Brewing Worldwide and the Irish Pub Company. The latter was founded in 1991 to design, fabricate, and install authentic Irish pubs worldwide.

The Dublin-based Irish Pub Company has built over 400 pubs in forty countries. The secret to their success? It's all about authentically re-creating the atmosphere one has come to expect when visiting a pub in Ireland, and that's where this company begins. First comes the design, of which there are five styles. The country cottage pub replicates a traditional stone building with thatched roof, rough timber beams, and whitewashed plaster walls; the traditional shop pub takes on the style of a grocery or hardware store that would have doubled as a pub in rural Ireland. Reminiscent of a Dublin city pub, the Victorian design is full of beveled mirrors and stained glass, while the Gaelic pub is styled with details from Celtic folklore and mythology. Finally, the brewery pub takes a page out of the design book of the famous St. James's Gate Brewery in Dublin and comes loaded with Guinness-inspired brewing memorabilia.

Once the design is selected and the pub is built, the Irish Pub Company consults on staff and management training, food and beverage requirements, and even provides a cookbook of sorts with recipes to give local products—such as sushi in Japan and pasta in Italy—an Irish flavor. For locations of Irish Pub Company pubs, see Resources, page 214.

· · · ·

GRACE NEILL'S, DONAGHADEE, COUNTY DOWN

Several Irish cheese makers produce goat cheese—St. Tola, Corleggy, and Corbetstown, to name a few. The cheeses come in creamy logs, button-like crottins, and firm, hard-rind varieties. Lightly fried goat cheese and mixed greens appear in many pub salads, but spicy rocket (arugula) and sweet roasted beets are a pleasant addition. Serve this with lusty mustard vinaigrette. **SERVES 4**

ROCKET, ROASTED BEETS, AND GOAT CHEESE SALAD
with Whole-Grain Mustard Vinaigrette

WHOLE-GRAIN MUSTARD VINAIGRETTE

1 tablespoon whole-grain mustard, preferably Lakeshore brand

1 tablespoon Dijon mustard

1 teaspoon honey

2 tablespoons white wine vinegar or white balsamic vinegar

½ cup extra virgin olive oil

½ teaspoon fresh lemon juice

Salt and freshly ground pepper to taste

SALAD

2 pounds small beets, washed

¼ cup extra virgin olive oil

1 teaspoon sea salt

Freshly ground black pepper

One 11-ounce log goat cheese, preferably Irish, cut into 8 rounds

1 cup walnuts, ground in a food processor

1 cup fresh white bread crumbs (see Note, page 33)

2 large egg yolks mixed with 2 tablespoons water

Canola oil for frying

1 large bunch rocket (arugula)

2 ounces mixed salad greens

⅔ cup walnuts, toasted (see Note, page 79)

1   **To make the vinaigrette:** In a small bowl, whisk together all the ingredients until well blended. Set aside.

2   **To start the salad:** Preheat the oven to 400°F. Place the beets in a baking dish, drizzle with the olive oil, and sprinkle with the sea salt and pepper. Toss to coat. Cover with foil and roast for 60 to 70 minutes, or until the beets are tender when pierced with a skewer. Remove from the oven, uncover, and let cool. When cool enough to handle, rub off the skins (see Note) and trim the roots. Cut into $^1/_4$-inch-thick slices, and cut the slices in half. Transfer the beets to a large bowl and toss with 2 to 3 tablespoons of the vinaigrette to coat.

3   Shape each round of cheese so it is $^1/_2$-inch thick. In a medium bowl, combine the ground nuts and bread crumbs. Put the egg wash in a small bowl. Dip each cheese round into the egg wash, then dredge in the bread crumb mixture, gently pressing on the crumbs and nuts to coat thoroughly. Place the rounds on a baking sheet and refrigerate for 30 minutes.

4   Heat 2 inches of the oil in a large skillet until very hot. Working in batches, cook the cheese for about 1 minute on each side, or until crisp and golden. With a slotted spoon, transfer the cheese to paper towels to drain.

5   **To compose the salads:** Divide the mixed greens among 4 salad plates. Arrange the beets over the greens, and top each serving with 2 rounds of cheese. Drizzle with the remaining vinaigrette and sprinkle with the walnuts.

NOTE: *To avoid staining your hands, use latex gloves while rubbing the skins off the beets.*

 ## DURTY NELLY, DAME ALICE, AND GRACE NEILL

Fast-talking, quick-witted, and ultra-friendly are some of the attributes you expect from a publican, an Irish barman who must be as adept at lending an ear as he is at pulling a pint. Not so with the ladies, it appears, especially those who have managed to assume a bit more than the role required and get themselves written into the pages of history as a bonus.

Durty Nelly, Dame Alice Le Kyteler, and Grace Neill are three of Ireland's most famous publicans, and their eponymous pubs attract crowds of tourists and locals alike.

Established in 1620, the Village Inn in Bunratty, County Clare, was named for "a robust lady, stately in stature, well-shaped, and with attributes which were genuine enough not to require any of the skillfully designed aids to the provocative beauty of the female form." She was known simply as Durty Nelly, a name that puzzled all who had the good fortune to be granted her welcome but were unaware of the story of struggle and heartbreak behind the warm smile of their contented hostess.

Times were hard in Ireland then, but Durty Nelly always seemed to manage quite well. She was keeper of the toll bridge over the river Owengarney, which flowed outside her window on its way to the Shannon. For those unable to pay the toll in cash, Nelly would accept just about anything, including a chicken, a few eggs, or a piece of home-cured bacon. She was also renowned for her little shebeen— a special corner of the house where a jar of whiskey was handled with expert care. Nelly eventually devised a primitive still to make her own, and she came up with the recipe for poitín (pronounced "potcheen"), a clear alcohol that is the Irish version of moonshine. Word quickly spread that "Durty Nelly had invented the great gift of new life; one that was good for all ages and for all ailments." She found fame and fortune in her house near the bridge, and her hospitality lives on in the popular pub next door to Bunratty Castle.

Dame Alice Le Kyteler was the original owner of Kyteler's Inn, on Kieran Street, in Kilkenny. Born there about 1263, she was the daughter of a Norman banker and was something of a sensation in her day. Possessing enough charm and wiles to acquire four husbands and considerable wealth, she managed to inflame the petty jealousies of those who eventually sought her downfall through charges of witchcraft. Along with various accomplices, Dame Alice was accused and brought to trial in 1324, and condemned to be whipped, dragged through the streets, and burned at the stake. Fortunately, she was able to escape this horrible fate with the help of some friends among the nobility, who evidently

conveyed her safely to England, where she disappeared from the pages of history. Not so her unfortunate maid, Petronella, who suffered the full measure of this medieval blood rite and was duly executed. It is now accepted that the charges against Dame Alice were trumped up by various enemies. Her house continues to be "a place of merrymaking and good cheer" however, or as some people like to say, "an inn altogether bewitching!"

Another well-known pub named for an Irishwoman is Grace Neill's, on High Street in Donaghadee, County Down. Originally known as the Kings Arms, it was renamed in the last century after its former landlady, Ms. Neill herself, who customarily greeted visitors to the inn with a welcoming kiss between puffs from her clay pipe. Her name is kept alive along with the assertion that her ghost haunts the building. Many members of the staff have witnessed unexplained events, ranging from the scattering of books and glasses in the bar to the switching on of kettles and the television. Sightings of a Victorian lady contained within a "puff of steam" have also been reported. The front bar of the pub remains virtually untouched from the days of Ms. Neill, and many tributes to her are tastefully displayed.

. . . .

GRACE NEILL'S, DONAGHADEE, COUNTY DOWN

Bulmers is Ireland's leading cider, a fermented drink often called "hard cider." In the United States, Bulmers is marketed as Magners, a brand name that can be traced back to the company's origins, when Willliam Magner started to ferment cider in Clonmel, County Tipperary. Magners brand has devised some recipes for publicans to showcase the increasingly popular drink, as it is a fine ingredient in foods as well. This scallop salad is one that is often featured as a blackboard special. **SERVES 4**

BLACKBOARD SPECIAL

WARM SCALLOP SALAD
with Cider Dressing

CIDER DRESSING

1½ cups Magners Irish cider or similar fermented cider

2 teaspoons Dijon mustard

⅓ cup sunflower oil

2 tablespoons hazelnut oil

Salt and freshly ground pepper to taste

SALAD

2 tablespoons extra virgin olive oil

2 pounds sea scallops

Salt and freshly ground pepper to taste

1 head Bibb or Boston lettuce, shredded

1 avocado, peeled and diced

2 Granny Smith apples, peeled, cored, and diced

1 tablespoon minced fresh flat-leaf parsley

1 tablespoon minced fresh dill

1 tablespoon minced fresh chives

Freshly ground pepper

1   **To make the dressing:** In a small saucepan over medium heat, bring the cider to a boil. Cook for 8 to 10 minutes, or until reduced by about two thirds. Remove from the heat and let cool for 5 minutes. Whisk in the mustard, sunflower oil, hazelnut oil, salt, and pepper. Set aside.

2   **To start the salad:** In a large skillet over medium heat, heat the oil. Cook the scallops, turning once or twice, for 2 to 3 minutes, or until opaque. Remove immediately from the heat and season with salt and pepper.

3   **To compose the salads:** In a large bowl, toss the lettuce, avocado, apples, parsley, dill, and chives with half the dressing. Divide into neat piles in the center of 4 salad plates and top with the scallops. Drizzle the remaining dressing on top and add a few grinds of pepper.

CHAPTER 4

HOT POTS, MEAT PIES, AND SAVORY TARTS

A hot pot, also known as "hotchpotch," is a rich, sometimes layered, vegetable and meat stew. The most popular version in Ireland is Irish stew. The late Theodora FitzGibbon, a renowned Irish cookery writer, said the dish is known "all over the Western world," and was originally made with potatoes, onions, and either mutton or kid because "no farmer would be so foolhardy as to use his lambs for it." She felt the flavor was spoiled if carrots or turnips were added, although today you might find one or both in what has become the quintessential Irish dish. The controversy doesn't stop with vegetables, however. There is little agreement on both the method of cooking (should the meat be browned; should it be cooked on top of the stove or in the oven?) and the meat (is mutton essential; should the lamb be boned or will chops do?). Brown soda bread, also a national treasure, and a glass of stout or dry red wine are the recommended accompaniments.

A meat pie is similar to a hot pot, but it is topped with a crust of either short-crust pastry or mashed potatoes. Both of these hearty dishes are extremely popular in pubs, along with more contemporary, often vegetarian, dishes such as savory tarts made with vegetables and cheese.

• • • • •

MAC'S PUB, BUNRATTY FOLK PARK, BUNRATTY, COUNTY CLARE

One of Ireland's earliest visitor attractions, Bunratty Folk Park, in Bunratty, County Clare, was developed to promote Irish heritage in a tourist environment. Founded by Shannon Development Company, the Folk Park is one of several visitor experiences and venues for entertainment in the Shannon area, including the renowned medieval castle banquets. Mac's Pub, which stands at the top of the main street in the reconstructed village, is a fine example of a Victorian hostelry, with a well-appointed "journeyman's dining room" and, of course, an inviting bar. The chef at Mac's deviates from Theodora FitzGibbon's directive (see page 91) by not only adding carrots to his Irish stew, but also celery and leeks. Serve it with Mac's Pub Brown Soda Bread. **SERVES 6**

MAC'S PUB IRISH STEW

2¼ pounds boneless lamb shoulder, cut into ½-inch pieces

1 pound lamb neck bones

6 cups homemade chicken stock (page 60), canned low-sodium chicken broth, or 6 chicken bouillon cubes mixed with 6 cups boiling water

3 medium potatoes, peeled and cut into 1-inch pieces

1 tablespoon minced fresh thyme

2 bay leaves

2 tablespoons minced fresh herbs, such as tarragon, marjoram, and rosemary

2 small onions, sliced

2 to 3 stalks celery, thickly sliced

2 leeks (white part only), washed and chopped

4 to 5 carrots, peeled and thickly sliced

Salt and freshly ground pepper to taste

Minced fresh flat-leaf parsley for garnish

Mac's Pub Brown Soda Bread for serving (facing page)

1 In a stockpot or large saucepan over medium heat, combine the lamb, bones, and stock or broth. Bring to a boil and skim off any foam that rises to the top. Reduce the heat to low, cover, and cook for 60 to 70 minutes, or until the meat is tender.

2 Add the potatoes, thyme, bay leaves, and herbs, return to a boil, reduce the heat, and simmer, uncovered, for 12 to 15 minutes, or until the potatoes are nearly tender. Add the onions, celery, leeks, and carrots and simmer for another 30 minutes. Uncover and cook for 15 to 20 minutes longer, or until the vegetables are tender and the stock has thickened. Season with salt and pepper.

3 To serve, ladle the stew into shallow bowls, sprinkle with parsley, and serve with Mac's Pub Brown Soda Bread.

Mac's Pub Brown Soda Bread   MAKES 1 LOAF

1 cup all-purpose flour

3 cups coarse whole wheat flour, such as Odlums or Howard's brand

1 tablespoon wheat germ

1 tablespoon oat bran, such as McCann's brand

1 tablespoon brown sugar

2 teaspoons baking soda

1 large egg

4 tablespoons unsalted Kerrygold Irish butter, melted

1½ to 1¾ cups buttermilk

2 tablespoons sesame seeds (optional)

1   Preheat the oven to 375°F. Butter and flour a 9-by-5-by-3-inch loaf pan.

2   In a large bowl, stir together the dry ingredients. Make a well in the center. With a wooden spoon, stir in the egg, melted butter, and 3/4 cup of the buttermilk. Mix well, and gradually add enough of the remaining buttermilk to form a soft dough.

3   Spoon the dough into the prepared pan, smooth the top with a spatula that has been dipped in water or buttermilk, and sprinkle with the sesame seeds, if using. Bake for 35 to 40 minutes, or until a skewer inserted in the center comes out clean and the bread sounds hollow when tapped on the bottom. Remove from the oven and let cool in the pan on a wire rack for 10 minutes. Turn the bread out onto the rack and let cool, right side up, for about 1 hour to make slicing easier.

One of Sligo's oldest pubs, Hargadon's, on O'Connell Street, adds barley to its stew to create a very rich, thick dish. Chef Gerard Reidy also offers his version of Hargadon's Brown Soda Bread, its natural accompaniment. **SERVES 6**

HARGADON'S IRISH STEW

2 pounds boneless lamb shoulder, cut into 1-inch pieces

2 cups barley

4 large carrots, peeled and thickly sliced

4 stalks celery, thickly sliced

3 onions, sliced

2 parsnips, peeled and sliced

5 potatoes, peeled and thickly sliced

Salt and freshly ground pepper to taste

Minced fresh flat-leaf parsley for garnish

Hargadon's Brown Soda Bread (page 98)

1   In a stockpot or large saucepan over medium heat, combine the lamb with enough water to cover. Bring to a boil and skim off any foam that rises to the top. Add the barley, reduce the heat to medium-low, and cook, covered, for 30 minutes, or until the meat is half tender. Stir in the carrots, celery, onion, parsnips, and potatoes, and season with salt and pepper. Cook for $1\frac{1}{2}$ to 2 hours, or until the meat and vegetables are tender and the stew is thickened.

2   To serve, ladle the stew into shallow bowls, sprinkle with parsley and serve with Hargadon's Brown Soda Bread.

CONTINUED

Hargadon's Brown Soda Bread   MAKES 1 LOAF

3 cups coarse whole-wheat flour, such as
  Odlums or Howard's brand

1 cup all-purpose flour

1 teaspoon baking soda

½ cup sugar

1 tablespoon salt

2 large eggs

1¼ cups buttermilk

1   Preheat the oven to 375°F. Butter and flour a 9-by-5-by-3-inch loaf pan.

2   In a large bowl, stir together the dry ingredients. Make a well in the center. In a small bowl, whisk together the eggs and buttermilk. With a wooden spoon, stir the egg mixture into the dry ingredients. Spoon the dough into the prepared pan and smooth the top with a spatula that has been dipped in water or buttermilk.

3   Bake for 35 to 40 minutes, or until a skewer inserted in the center comes out clean and the bread sounds hollow when tapped on the bottom. Remove from the oven and let cool in the pan on a wire rack for 10 minutes. Turn the bread out onto the rack and let cool, right side up, for about 1 hour to make slicing easier.

 **BLOOMSDAY**

As part of his daylong wanderings through Dublin in James Joyce's *Ulysses,* Leopold Bloom visited Davy Byrne's Pub for a lunch of Gorgonzola cheese and a glass of Burgundy. The day was June 16, 1904, and for Joyce admirers, June 16 has come to be known as "Bloomsday." It's celebrated with great relish by Dubliners, who retrace Bloom's odyssey each year, and by Joyce fans around the globe, who hold Bloomsday readings and improvise scenes from the novel.

For many in Dublin, it's one big parade. Some Joyce devotees appear in Edwardian dress, others as Joyce himself or as one of the characters, including Aeolus, the Lestrygonians, and Wandering Rocks. The parade, like the book, starts at the round Martello Tower, now the James Joyce Museum, in Sandycove, and snakes its way through fine and dingy streets to sites mentioned by Joyce, including Sweny's, a chemist's shop just behind the playing fields of Trinity College, and Davy Byrne's on Duke Street. Dubliners celebrated the one hundredth anniversary of Bloomsday in 2004, but as poet Brendan Behan once said, "In Dublin, every day is 'Bloomsday'." For details, see Resources, page 214.

· · · ·

THE DUKE, DUBLIN

Coddle is a hearty pork, potato, and sausage stew that is found on many pub menus, especially in the Dublin area. Popular since the eighteenth century, it was traditionally served for Saturday night supper. This recipe, adapted from one served at Oliver St. John Gogarty's, on Fleet Street in Dublin's popular Temple Bar district, is heartwarming fare for cold-weather nights. **SERVES 4**

DUBLIN CODDLE

12 ounces Irish pork sausages

4 ounces lean pork, cut into 1-inch pieces

8 ounces Irish boiling bacon (shoulder or collar; see page 53), cut into 2-inch pieces

2 onions, sliced

3 medium potatoes, peeled and thickly sliced

3 tablespoons minced fresh flat-leaf parsley

2 sprigs fresh thyme

Freshly ground pepper to taste

1 Prick the sausages in several places with a fork. Put the sausages, pork, and bacon in a large saucepan over medium heat and add enough cold water to cover. Bring to a boil, then reduce the heat to medium-low, and simmer for 10 to 15 minutes, or until the bacon is slightly tender. Skim off any foam that rises. Drain, reserving the liquid.

2 Preheat the oven to 350°F. Arrange half the meat in the bottom of a Dutch oven or ovenproof casserole. In layers add half the onions and then half the potatoes. Sprinkle with some parsley, thyme, and pepper. Repeat the layers, beginning with the remaining meat and ending with the remaining herbs and a sprinkling of pepper. Pour the reserved cooking liquid over all. Top with a sheet of waxed paper, then cover with the pot lid. Bake for 1 to 1 1/2 hours, or until the potatoes are tender. Serve immediately.

Another perennial pub favorite is a hot pot made with beef and Guinness stout. It can be cooked as a stewlike casserole, as in this recipe from the Brewery Bar at the Guinness Storehouse, St. James's Gate, in Dublin (see page 191), or as a meat pie (page 102). At the Storehouse, this dish is served with a big scoop of mashed potatoes in the center and a sprinkling of parsley, but you can also serve it with a few boiled potatoes, if you like. SERVES 6

GUINNESS BEEF STEW

2 pounds boneless beef sirloin, cut into 1-inch cubes

Salt and freshly ground pepper to taste

All-purpose flour for dredging

4 tablespoons unsalted Kerrygold Irish butter

¼ cup canola oil

4 medium onions, chopped

2 cups homemade beef stock (page 61), canned low-sodium beef broth, or 2 beef bouillon cubes mixed with 2 cups boiling water

2 cups Guinness stout

5 carrots, peeled and thickly sliced

4 parsnips, peeled and thickly sliced

1 medium turnip, peeled and cut into 1-inch pieces

Mashed or boiled potatoes for serving

1 Season the meat with salt and pepper and dredge in flour. In a stockpot or large saucepan over medium heat, melt the butter with the oil. Working in batches, cook the meat on all sides for 5 to 7 minutes, or until evenly browned. Remove from the pot. Stir in the onions and cook for 3 to 5 minutes, or until soft.

2 Return all the meat to the pot and add enough of the beef stock or broth and the Guinness to cover. Bring to a boil, reduce the heat to medium-low, cover, and simmer for 60 to 70 minutes, or until the meat is nearly tender. Add the carrots, parsnips, and turnip, and cook for 30 to 40 minutes, or until the vegetables and meat are tender and the stew is thickened. (If not thick enough, mix 2 tablespoons flour with ½ cup of water until smooth. Stir into the stew and cook for 5 minutes longer, or until it reaches the desired consistency.)

3 To serve, ladle the stew into shallow bowls and serve with potatoes.

Davy Byrnes, on Duke Street, is one of Dublin's most famous pubs and has long been associated with James Joyce's novel *Ulysses* (see page 99). The chef uses a traditional recipe for Guinness beef stew as the basis for a meat pie and tops it with homemade pastry. The pie is certainly hearty pub fare, but it's also a great dish to serve company at home since the stew can be prepared a day in advance. The crust comes together quickly in a food processor and is added just before baking. The beef needs to marinate for a day before it's cooked, so plan accordingly. **SERVES 6 TO 8**

BEEF AND GUINNESS PIE

FILLING

2 pounds stewing beef, cut into ½-inch pieces

4 cups Guinness stout

1 clove garlic

2 bay leaves, split

1 cup homemade beef stock (page 61), canned low-sodium beef broth, or 1 beef bouillon cube mixed with 1 cup boiling water

2 stalks celery, sliced

2 large carrots, peeled and sliced

1 large onion, sliced

Salt and freshly ground pepper to taste

2 tablespoons minced fresh flat-leaf parsley

1 bouquet garni (a cheesecloth bag containing 3 sprigs fresh parsley, 1 sprig fresh thyme, 8 to 10 black peppercorns, and 1 bay leaf)

1 tablespoon cornstarch

½ cup cold water

3 to 4 large mushrooms, sliced (optional)

PASTRY

1¾ cups all-purpose flour

Pinch of salt

⅓ cup solid vegetable shortening, such as Crisco

⅓ cup unsalted Kerrygold Irish butter, cut into small pieces

⅓ cup ice water

1 egg mixed with 1 tablespoon water

1   **To start the filling:** In a large bowl or nonreactive pot, combine the beef, 2 cups of the Guinness, the garlic, and bay leaves. Cover and refrigerate for 24 hours. Drain the marinade and discard the garlic and bay leaf.

2   In a stockpot or large saucepan over medium heat, bring the marinated beef, the remaining 2 cups of Guinness, and the beef stock or broth to a boil. Reduce the heat to medium-low, cover, and simmer for 1 to 1 1/2 hours, or until the meat is tender. Skim off any foam that rises to the top. Add the celery, carrots, onion, salt, pepper, parsley, and bouquet garni and cook for 15 to 20 minutes, or until the vegetables are slightly tender. In a small bowl, combine the cornstarch with 1/2 cup of cold water, and whisk until smooth. Stir into the filling, and cook for 2 to 3 minutes, or until the liquid is thickened.

3   **To make the pastry:** Combine the flour, salt, shortening, and butter in a food processor fitted with a metal blade. Pulse 4 to 5 times, or until the mixture resembles coarse crumbs. Sprinkle in 4 tablespoons of the water, pulse 4 to 5 times, and if needed, add the rest of the water and pulse again. Wrap the dough in plastic wrap and refrigerate for 30 minutes. On a floured surface, roll out the dough to a circle 12 inches in diameter.

4   Preheat the oven to 375°F. Remove the bouquet garni, and transfer the filling to a 10-inch deep-dish pie plate. Stir in the mushrooms, if using. Cover with the pastry, crimp the edges, and cut a few slits in the top to allow steam to escape. Brush the top with the egg wash. Bake for 30 to 35 minutes, or until the top is golden and the mixture is bubbling.

In a land where sheep are so plentiful, it's not surprising that lamb is the foundation for many farmhouse and pub dishes. Shepherd's pie, a longtime favorite, was originally created as an economical way to use leftover lamb and was always a favorite with farmers. When the pie is made with beef, it's called "cottage pie." Both are generally topped with a crust of mashed potatoes rather than pastry. **SERVES 4**

SHEPHERD'S PIE

FILLING

3 tablespoons canola oil

2 pounds ground lamb

Salt and freshly ground pepper

1 medium onion, chopped

2 carrots, peeled and diced

2 tablespoons minced fresh flat-leaf parsley

1 teaspoon minced fresh thyme

1½ tablespoons all-purpose flour

3 cups homemade beef stock (page 61), canned low-sodium beef broth, or 3 bouillon cubes mixed with 3 cups boiling water

TOPPING

2 pounds russet potatoes, peeled and cut into 1-inch pieces

½ cup milk

2 tablespoons unsalted Kerrygold Irish butter

3 tablespoons Cheddar cheese, preferably Irish, grated (optional)

1 **To start the filling:** In a large skillet over medium heat, warm 2 tablespoons of the oil. Add the lamb and cook for 5 to 7 minutes, or until browned. Season with salt and pepper. Remove from the heat, and with a slotted spoon, transfer the meat to a large bowl.

2   Add the remaining 1 tablespoon of oil to the pan. Stir in the onion and cook for 3 to 5 minutes, or until the onion is soft but not browned. Add the carrots, parsley, and thyme, and cook, stirring once or twice, for 2 to 3 minutes, or until the vegetables are coated with oil. Stir in the flour, cook for 1 to 2 minutes, then add the stock or broth. Bring to a boil, scraping up the browned bits from the bottom of the pan. Add the meat, reduce the heat to low, and simmer, uncovered, stirring occasionally, for 20 to 25 minutes, or until the lamb is tender and the sauce is thickened. Season again with salt and pepper.

3   Preheat the oven to 425°F.

4   **To make the topping:** In a large saucepan over medium heat, cook the potatoes in boiling salted water for 12 to 15 minutes, or until tender. Drain and mash. Add the milk and butter and stir until smooth.

5   Transfer the stew to a large casserole dish or 4 individual ovenproof casserole dishes. Decoratively spread or pipe the mashed potatoes over the meat mixture and bake for 10 to 12 minutes, or until the mixture is hot. Preheat the broiler for just a few minutes and sprinkle the potatoes with the grated cheese, if using. Place the pie under the preheated broiler, 4 inches from the heat source, and broil for 1 to 2 minutes, or until the potatoes are lightly browned and the cheese is bubbling.

The Old Stand, on Exchequer Street in Dublin, is one of the oldest public houses in Ireland. In 1659, Charles II renewed its public house license, and there is evidence that a license existed even 200 years before on this exact location at the corner of Exchequer and St. Andrews streets, an intersection important in both Viking and Medieval days. Today the pub is popular with rugby fans and racing enthusiasts, bankers, brokers, and barristers who relish its hot lunches—chicken and ham pie, deep-fried scampi, and gorgeous steaks—as well as classic fish salads, open-face sandwiches, and good wines. The chef's recipe for chicken and ham pie also makes a delicious filling for vol-au-vents, cup-shaped puff pastry shells with lids that are filled with a creamy mixture of chicken, seafood, or vegetables. They are popular in Irish pubs (see the variation that follows). **SERVES 6**

CHICKEN AND HAM PIE

4 tablespoons unsalted Kerrygold Irish butter

¼ cup all-purpose flour

2 cups homemade chicken stock (page 60), canned low-sodium chicken broth, or 2 chicken bouillon cubes mixed with 2 cups boiling water

½ cup half-and-half

¼ cup chopped onion

4 ounces white mushrooms, sliced

1 cup fresh or frozen peas

2 tablespoons minced fresh flat-leaf parsley

1 cup cooked chicken, cut into ½-inch pieces

1 cup cooked ham, diced

Salt and freshly ground pepper

1 sheet frozen puff pastry from a 17.3-ounce package, left at room temperature for 30 minutes (see Note)

1 large egg beaten with 1 tablespoon water

1   Preheat the oven to 375°F. Butter a 10-inch deep-dish pie plate.

2   In a medium saucepan over medium heat, melt the butter. Whisk in the flour and cook for 1 to 2 minutes, or until blended with the butter. Add the stock or broth and cook, whisking constantly, for 2 to 3 minutes, or until the mixture comes to a boil. Reduce the heat and simmer gently for 2 to 3 minutes, or until the sauce starts to thicken. Stir in the half-and-half, onion, mushrooms, peas, and parsley, and cook for 3 to 5 minutes, or until the vegetables are nearly tender. Add the chicken and ham and season with salt and pepper. Spoon the mixture into the prepared dish.

3 Unfold the pastry on a lightly floured surface. Roll out into a circle 12 inches in diameter. Place the pastry over the chicken mixture, trim, and crimp the edges. Cut a few slits in the top to allow steam to escape. Brush with egg wash and bake for 20 to 25 minutes, or until the pastry is puffed and golden. Remove the pie from the oven and let cool for 5 minutes on a wire rack before serving.

VARIATION:

To make chicken and ham vol-au-vents, omit the puff pastry sheets and use 6 frozen puff pastry shells, such as Pepperidge Farm brand. Preheat the oven to 400°F. Place the pastry shells about 2 inches apart on an ungreased baking sheet with the tops facing up. Bake for 20 to 25 minutes, or until golden brown. Use a fork to remove the tops and soft pastry underneath. Spoon the hot chicken and ham mixture into the shells and return to the oven for 3 to 5 minutes for extra crispness. Set the lids on top of the filling for serving.

NOTE: *Reserve the remaining sheet of puff pastry for another use by wrapping it well in plastic and storing it in the freezer.*

Known in Irish as "An Muileann," the Mills Inn was established in 1755 in Ballyvourney, County Cork, where my great-grandfather Daniel Crowley was born in 1822. The inn, with pub and roadside gift shop, derives its name from the grain mill and flax tucking mills that were on the banks of the nearby Sullane River. Today the Mills Inn, located on the main Cork to Killarney road, is a popular stopover for visitors touring this scenic part of Ireland. It's also a haven for locals in this *Gaeltacht* (Irish-speaking) region. Known for its hearty food, the pub serves this beef and pepper dish as an alternative to a traditional beef hot pot. Serve it with Cheddar-Herb Biscuits. **SERVES 4**

BEEF AND VEGETABLE PEPPER POT

2 tablespoons olive oil

1 pound beef tenderloin, cut into thin strips

1 red onion, sliced and cut into thin strips

½ Spanish onion, sliced and cut into thin strips

1 clove garlic, minced

½ red pepper, seeded, deribbed, and cut into thin strips

½ green pepper, seeded, deribbed, and cut into thin strips

2 stalks celery, cut crosswise into 2-inch lengths and lengthwise into thin strips

2 tablespoons tomato paste

2 cups homemade beef stock (page 61), canned low-sodium beef broth, or 2 beef bouillon cubes mixed with 2 cups boiling water

Salt and freshly ground pepper to taste

Minced fresh flat-leaf parsley for garnish

Cheddar-Herb Biscuits for serving (page 110)

1   In a large, deep skillet over medium heat, warm the oil. Cook the beef for 3 to 4 minutes, or until browned. With a slotted spoon, transfer the beef to a plate and set aside. Add the onions and garlic to the skillet and cook for 3 to 4 minutes, or until lightly browned. Add the peppers, celery, tomato paste, stock or broth, salt, and pepper. Bring to a boil, then reduce the heat to medium-low and simmer for 15 to 20 minutes, or until the peppers are tender and the sauce is thickened. Stir in the beef and cook until heated through.

2   To serve, ladle into shallow bowls and sprinkle with parsley, with Cheddar-Herb Biscuits on the side.

CONTINUED

Cheddar-Herb Biscuits   MAKES 1 DOZEN

2½ cups all-purpose flour

2 tablespoons sugar

1 tablespoon baking powder

¾ teaspoon cream of tartar

½ teaspoon salt

½ cup (1 stick) unsalted Kerrygold Irish butter, cut into pieces, plus extra for serving

4 ounces (1 cup) Kerrygold Vintage or other aged cheddar, grated

2 tablespoons minced fresh herbs, such as parsley, rosemary, and tarragon

1 large egg

1¼ cups buttermilk

1 Preheat the oven to 400°F. Butter a 12-cup (¹/₃-cup capacity) muffin pan.

2 Combine the dry ingredients in a food processor fitted with a metal blade. Pulse 2 to 3 times to blend. Add the butter and process for 10 to 15 seconds, or until the mixture resembles coarse crumbs. Add the cheese and herbs and pulse again 2 to 3 times to blend. Add the egg and buttermilk, and process for 10 to 20 seconds, or until a soft dough forms.

3 Spoon the batter into the muffin cups and bake for 20 to 23 minutes, or until the biscuits are lightly browned and a skewer inserted in the center comes out clean. Serve warm with butter.

GUINNESS OSCARS AND BLACK AND WHITE PUB AWARDS

It's not exactly the Academy Awards, but almost—especially if you're a publican in Northern Ireland, where Guinness Oscars are handed out annually for the province's top pubs. Each year five winners are chosen from a list of outstanding pubs, but only the best of the best are selected from these four categories: best pub front, best charitable event promotion, best pub personality, and best overall bar.

In the Republic, the best pubs are honored with Black and White pub awards in a national competition. Sponsored by Edward Dillon and Company, a Dublin wine and spirits distributor, the awards are the foremost and most coveted within the Irish licensed trade. They've been given for nearly thirty years, recognizing excellence in pubs and hotel bars. Pubs are judged on atmosphere and a welcoming interior, staff efficiency and friendliness, cleanliness, exterior appearance, and a well-served range of drinks. Surprisingly, food is not part of the judging criteria since many pubs are involved solely in the "wet trade." But in most cases, the top pubs in each province (Leinster, Munster, Connaught) serve traditional pub food. In addition to the provincial winners, one is chosen as "Pub of the Year" and there are awards for "Superpub," "Hotel Bar of the Year," "Newcomer of the Year," and "National Heritage Pub." For details, see Resources, page 214.

. . . .

MOLLY DARCY'S PUB, KILLARNEY, COUNTY KERRY

Ken and Cathleen Buggy's Glencairn Inn, outside Lismore, in County Waterford, is an extraordinary pub, known as much for its originality in cooking as for its old-fashioned charm. The inn, which doubles as a bed-and-breakfast, has three dining areas: a cozy breakfast room, an atmospheric old kitchen, and a quaint pub. Everything in the pub is "made on the day," so if tomatoes are in season, they might turn up in salads, soups, and tarts—such as this one made with green tomatoes. Food writer John McKenna, a fan of Ken Buggy's cooking, says: "On the surface, everything seems simple, sober, straightforward. But his cooking is different from anyone else's and works out of a different flavor perspective." This delightful dish is perfect for a late summer's lunch or starter. **SERVES 4 TO 6**

GREEN TOMATO TARTE TATIN

¼ cup extra virgin olive oil

2 tablespoons light brown sugar

6 medium green tomatoes, cut in half

Salt and freshly ground pepper to taste

1 sheet frozen puff pastry from a 17.3-ounce package, left at room temperature for 30 minutes (see Note)

1 egg beaten with 1 tablespoon water

2 to 3 tablespoons minced fresh basil, plus whole basil leaves for garnish

Grated Parmesan cheese for sprinkling on tart

Mixed green salad for serving (optional)

1 In a 10-inch round ovenproof skillet, heat the oil over medium-high heat. Stir in the brown sugar. Season the tomatoes with salt and pepper and place them, cut side down, in the skillet. Fry, without turning, for 4 to 5 minutes, or until caramelized. To stop the cooking process, remove the skillet from the heat and place in a large pan filled with enough ice water to come halfway up the sides of the skillet.

2 Unfold the pastry on a lightly floured surface. Roll into a circle 12 inches in diameter. Place the pastry over the tomatoes, tucking it around the edges of the pan. Refrigerate for 20 minutes.

3   Preheat the oven to 425°F. Brush the pastry with the egg mixture and bake the tart for 15 to 20 minutes, or until the pastry is puffed and golden. Place a rimmed serving plate over the pan. With pot holders to protect your hands, invert the tart onto the plate and remove the skillet. Sprinkle the tomatoes with the minced basil and cheese. Let the tart rest for 5 minutes.

4   To serve, cut the tart into slices and garnish with the basil leaves. Serve warm or cold with a mixed green salad, if desired.

NOTE: *Reserve the remaining sheet of puff pastry for another use by wrapping it well in plastic and storing it in the freezer.*

Barry's, located in the village of Douglas, a suburb of Cork City, was named the Black and White "Pub of the Year" in 2003 (see page 111). Not your average country pub by any means, the ultra-contemporary bar and restaurant was first established in 1776, when it was known as the Tramway House because of the stopovers made by coaches on their way to Cork City. Two major renovations in recent years have transformed the premises into one of the area's most attractive and popular establishments, earning it honors for provincial and national Superpub of the Year in addition to the ultimate accolade of top pub in Ireland. **SERVES 4**

FOUR-CHEESE TORTE
with Tomato, Pepper, and Pesto

2 sheets frozen puff pastry from a 17.3-ounce package, left at room temperature for 30 minutes

1 large egg mixed with 2 tablespoons water

2 ounces Cashel Blue cheese, or another blue cheese, crumbled

2 ounces Kerrygold Vintage Cheddar, or another aged Cheddar, cut into small pieces

2 ounces mozzarella cheese, cut into small pieces

2 ounces sun-dried tomatoes, cut into small pieces

½ red pepper, seeded, deribbed, and thinly sliced

2 ounces St. Tola goat cheese, or another goat cheese, cut into 4 slices

2 tablespoons prepared pesto or basil dressing (page 139)

Rocket (arugula) for garnish

1   Preheat the oven to 325°F. Line a baking sheet with parchment paper.

2   Unfold the pastry sheets on a lightly floured surface. Roll each out into a 12-inch square. Brush one sheet with egg wash, then place the second sheet on top. Cut the doubled sheet into quarters, and brush the top layer of each one with the egg wash. With a serrated knife, score the top of the small squares corner-to-corner, cutting through the top sheet, only, to create an X. Starting at the center, pull back each piece to create a star shape.

3   In a large bowl, combine the blue cheese, Cheddar, mozzarella, tomatoes, and pepper. Toss to mix. Fill the center of each of the squares with the cheese mixture, and put a slice of goat cheese in the center. Transfer to the baking sheet and bake for 20 minutes, or until the pastry is puffed and golden and the cheeses are melted. Remove from the oven and let cool on a wire rack for 5 minutes.

4   To serve, drizzle each torte with pesto or basil dressing, and garnish with a few sprigs of rocket.

Nettles grow wildly and profusely in Ireland in the spring, and they're a popular ingredient in savory dishes like soups and tarts. At Molly Darcy's Pub, the Black and White "Pub of the Year" winner in 1992, chef Eileen O'Brien suggests substituting spinach for the nettles if you don't live where they grow. Molly Darcy's is part of the Muckross Park Hotel, established in 1795 in the heart of Killarney's national park in County Kerry. The traditional pub sports wooden floors, stone walls, beamed ceilings, open fires, a friendly atmosphere, and fine Irish fare. **SERVES 6**

Caramelized Onion and
NETTLE TARTS

CRUST

1 cup whole wheat flour

¼ cup all-purpose flour

¼ teaspoon salt

¼ teaspoon sugar

6 tablespoons unsalted Kerrygold Irish butter, cut into small pieces

½ cup buttermilk

FILLING

8 ounces nettles or spinach, washed and trimmed

3 tablespoons extra virgin olive oil

1 cup chopped onions

2 tablespoons sugar

2 tablespoons dry white wine

4 large eggs

1½ cups heavy (whipping) cream

Salt and freshly ground pepper to taste

Tomato wedges for garnish

1   **To start the crust:** Combine the flours, salt, sugar, and butter in a food processor fitted with a metal blade. Pulse 8 to 10 times, or until the mixture resembles coarse crumbs. Add the buttermilk and process for 20 to 25 seconds, or until a soft dough forms. Shape the dough into a ball, wrap it in plastic wrap, and refrigerate for 30 minutes.

2   **To make the filling:** Working in batches, combine the nettles or spinach with 2 tablespoons of the olive oil in a clean food processor or blender. Process for 8 to 10 seconds, or until smooth.

3   In a large skillet over medium heat, warm the remaining 1 tablespoon of the oil. Stir in the onions and sugar and cook for 5 to 7 minutes, or until the onions begin to caramelize. Stir in the wine and continue to cook for 3 to 5 minutes, or until the wine is nearly evaporated.

4   In a large bowl, beat the eggs and cream with an electric mixer for 2 to 3 minutes, or until well blended. Season with salt and pepper.

5   Preheat the oven to 350°F. Butter a 12-cup muffin pan.

6   Cut the dough in half. On a floured surface, roll out each half to a circle 12 inches in diameter. With a 3-inch cookie cutter, cut out 6 circles from each half. Press a circle of dough into each of the muffin cups. Spread some of the nettle or spinach mixture onto each crust, spoon the onions on top, and fill each cup with some of the egg mixture. Bake for 25 to 30 minutes, or until the fillings are set and the tops are brown. Remove from the oven and let cool on a wire rack for 5 minutes.

7   To serve, gently lift out the tarts from the pans with an offset spatula. Place 2 tarts on each of 6 salad plates, and garnish with tomatoes.

Clonakilty, in scenic West Cork, has been synonymous with black pudding since Philip Harrington developed a recipe for it at his butcher shop on Sovereign Street (now Pearse Street) in the 1890s. Years later, Edward Twomey took over the shop and the recipe from Harrington, and today the Clonakilty brand remains Ireland's best known. At An Súgán, a pub and restaurant a short distance from Twomey's, the O'Crowley family likes to include it on the menu in a variety of ways, including this risotto, often one of their daily specials. SERVES 4

BLACKBOARD SPECIAL

Mushroom Risotto with
CLONAKILTY BLACK PUDDING

2 tablespoons canola oil

1 black pudding, cut into ½-inch-thick slices

6 cups homemade chicken stock (page 60), canned low-sodium chicken broth, or 6 chicken bouillon cubes mixed with 6 cups boiling water

½ cup (1 stick) plus 2 tablespoons unsalted Kerrygold Irish butter

1 tablespoon extra virgin olive oil

3 shallots, minced

8 ounces white mushrooms, sliced

1 cup Arborio rice

Salt and freshly ground pepper to taste

1   In a large skillet over medium heat, warm the oil. Fry the slices of pudding for 3 to 4 minutes on each side, or until browned. Cut each slice in half and set aside.

2   In a medium saucepan over medium heat, bring the stock or broth to a boil. Reduce the heat to low and keep warm.

3   In a large skillet over medium heat, melt the butter with the olive oil. Add the shallots and cook for 2 to 3 minutes, or until soft but not browned. Add the mushrooms and cook for 2 to 3 minutes, or until tender. Add the rice and stir until coated with the butter. Add the warm stock, ¼ cup at a time, and stir constantly to prevent the rice from sticking to the pan. When the rice has absorbed the liquid, add another ¼ cup. Continue adding the stock and stirring for 20 to 25 minutes, or until all the stock has been used. Stir in the pudding, season with salt and pepper, and cook for 1 to 2 minutes, or until the pudding is heated through.

CHAPTER 5

MEAT AND POTATOES

Honest, wholesome, and down-to-earth food has always been the hallmark of an Irish pub. Many pride themselves on their daily "carvery," a hot buffet where the centerpiece is a carved-on-the-spot joint of meat, such as ham, leg of lamb, or roast pork served with a variety of potatoes and vegetables. Traditional dishes like Bacon and Cabbage (page 125) and Irish stew (pages 94 and 97) are usually on offer, too. When the menu is longer, you can be assured of hearty cooked-to-order steaks and chops and interesting dishes made with chicken and duck, accompanied by potatoes, potatoes, and more of the same.

• • • • •

FIDDLER'S GREEN, PORTAFERRY, COUNTY DOWN

Second only to Irish stew, bacon and cabbage is one of Ireland's most traditional dishes. Parsley Sauce or Whole-Grain Mustard Sauce (page 126) is the usual accompaniment, along with boiled potatoes and often turnip and carrots. **SERVES 4 TO 6**

BACON AND CABBAGE

3 pounds Irish boiling bacon (shoulder or collar; see page 53)

1 small head cabbage, cored and quartered

Parsley Sauce or Whole-Grain Mustard Sauce for serving (page 126)

Boiled potatoes for serving

1 Put the bacon in a large saucepan and cover with cold water. Bring the water slowly to a boil, then cover and reduce the heat to medium-low. Simmer, skimming the water occasionally to remove the foam, for 1 1/2 hours (about 30 minutes per pound), or until the meat is tender when pierced with a fork.

2 About 20 minutes before the bacon is cooked, add the cabbage. Cook for 15 to 20 minutes, or until the cabbage is tender, but not soggy. Transfer the bacon to a serving dish, and let cool for 10 minutes before slicing. Drain the cabbage, reserving 1/4 cup of the cooking liquid for the Parsley Sauce or 1 1/2 cups for the Whole-Grain Mustard Sauce, and transfer to a serving dish.

3 To serve, slice the meat and serve it with the cabbage, potatoes, and sauce.

CONTINUED

Parsley Sauce   MAKES ABOUT 1½ CUPS

4 tablespoons unsalted Kerrygold Irish butter

3 tablespoons all-purpose flour

¼ cup bacon cooking liquid

1¼ cups hot milk

Salt and freshly ground pepper to taste

½ cup minced fresh flat-leaf parsley

In a small saucepan over medium heat, melt the butter. Gradually stir in the flour. Cook for 1 to 2 minutes, or until blended. Slowly stir in the cooking liquid, then the milk. Bring to a boil and cook, whisking constantly, for 3 to 5 minutes, or until slightly thickened. Add the salt, pepper, and parsley and cook, whisking constantly, for 3 to 5 minutes more, or until the sauce is smooth. Serve warm.

Whole-Grain Mustard Sauce   MAKES ABOUT 2 CUPS

2 tablespoons unsalted Kerrygold Irish butter

1 small onion, chopped

1 clove garlic, minced

2 teaspoons whole-grain mustard

⅔ cup dry white wine

1¼ cups bacon cooking liquid, plus more as needed

1¼ cups half-and-half, plus more as needed

Salt and freshly ground pepper to taste

In a saucepan, melt the butter over medium heat. Add the onion and garlic and cook for 5 minutes, or until soft. Stir in the mustard and wine and cook for 2 minutes. Add the cooking liquid and half-and-half and cook, whisking constantly, for 5 to 7 minutes, or until reduced by half. Add the salt and pepper and cook for 5 minutes, or until the mixture has a creamy consistency. Add more boiling liquid or half-and-half, if needed, to make a smooth sauce. Serve warm.

O'Neill's Public House, on Suffolk Street in Dublin, has been licensed for over 300 years. This area of Dublin has played a vital commercial and cultural role in the formation of the city's history from Viking times to the present day, and its close proximity to Trinity College and Dublin Castle has made it an inviting residential location. Today, the busy pub is situated in the heart of the city, directly opposite Dublin Tourism Center and steps away from pedestrianized Grafton Street and trendy Temple Bar. The pub is renowned for its reasonably priced carvery lunches (served daily from noon to 7:00 P.M.) and the ageless character of its interior space, with countless alcoves, snugs, nooks, and crannies. One of the most popular items from the carvery is this baked Limerick ham, an Irish cured ham traditionally smoked over juniper branches and berries to produce a distinctive flavor (see Resources, page 214). Serve it with Parsley Sauce (facing page) and Mashed Potatoes (page 146). **SERVES 4 TO 6**

BAKED LIMERICK HAM

One 4- to 5-pound Irish cured ham (see Note)	1 cup dark brown sugar
¾ cup Dijon mustard	1 cup honey
About 25 whole cloves	Parsley Sauce (facing page) for serving

1   Put the ham in a Dutch oven and cover with cold water. Bring the water slowly to a boil, then cover and reduce the heat to medium-low. Simmer, skimming the water occasionally to remove any foam that rises, for 1 to 1 1/2 hours (about 20 minutes per pound), or until the meat is tender when pierced with a fork. Remove from the heat and let the meat sit in the cooking liquid for 30 minutes.

2   Preheat the oven to 325°F. Remove the meat from the liquid and transfer to a large baking pan. With a sharp knife, skin and score the fat in a diamond pattern, cover with the mustard, and stud with a whole clove in the center of each diamond. Sprinkle with brown sugar and drizzle with honey. Bake for 30 to 35 minutes, or until the ham is golden. Remove from the oven and let rest for 20 minutes before carving.

3   Slice the ham and serve it with mashed potatoes and Parsley Sauce.

NOTE: *In Ireland, only the leg of the pig is called "ham" (and also "gammon"); otherwise, the meat is "bacon" (see page 53).*

THE CROWN LIQUOR SALOON, BELFAST

The Crown Liquor Saloon, also known as the Crown Bar, is both ageless and priceless. A gem of Victoriana, it is undoubtedly one of the finest bars in the world. Located at 46 Great Victoria Street, on Belfast's Golden Mile, the Crown is an outstanding example of the Victorian gin palaces that once flourished in the industrial cities of Britain. Wonderfully preserved, the Crown is cherished by the people of Belfast, visited by thousands of tourists each year, and so revered as an institution that the National Trust has owned it since 1978, when Sir John Betjeman, the late English poet laureate, convinced the Trust to take it over. In 1981, the Trust carried out a sympathetic restoration to restore it to its full Victorian splendor.

Among the unusual artistic touches in the bar are scalloped gaslights; a burnished primrose, yellow, and gold ceiling; a floor laid out in a myriad of mosaic tiles; brocaded walls covered in patterned tiles; unusual wood carvings; ornate mirrors; and wooden columns with Corinthian capitals and feather motifs in gold. Painted and etched glass is everywhere, vivid with painted shells, fairies, pineapples, and fleurs-de-lis. The long Balmoral red granite–topped bar is divided by columns and faced with colored tiles. A heated footrest adds another touch of luxury. Boldly emblazoned on the mahogany cabinet behind the bar, the Crown boasts: "High Class Whiskey, Direct Importers, Special Wines."

Aside from its elaborate interior design, the Crown also features ten differently shaped and elaborately carved snugs, or wooden booths, lettered from A to J. Their most popular features are the gunmetal plate each one has for striking matches, and an antique bell system, which alerts the bar staff to their customers' liquid needs. A feature of many traditional pubs, drinking snugs were not originally built for comfort, but to accommodate those who preferred to slip in for a quick one and drink quietly and unseen. For those who want to be seen, however, the Crown has recently installed a decidedly modern innovation, a Web camera, greatly favored by tourists, who can wave to the folks at home! For additional details on the Crown, see Resources, page 214.

. . . .

THE CROWN LIQUOR SALOON, BELFAST

The Crown Liquor Saloon, on Great Victoria Street in Belfast, is one of the greatest bars in the world (see page 128), with an ornate Victorian interior and a red granite–topped bar. Dining in one of the carved wooden snugs is a special treat. The pub/restaurant is known for serving delicious traditional meals such as Bacon and Cabbage (page 125), sausage and mash, and this leek-laden chicken dish with bacon and cream. Serve this with Garlic Mash (page 146). **SERVES 4**

ROAST CHICKEN
with Bacon and Leeks

2 tablespoons unsalted Kerrygold Irish butter at room temperature

3 pounds cut-up chicken

Salt and freshly ground pepper to taste

1 tablespoon sunflower oil

8 ounces Irish boiling bacon (shoulder or collar; see page 53), cut into ½-inch pieces

1 pound leeks (white part only), washed and sliced

1 cup homemade chicken stock (page 60), canned low-sodium chicken broth, or 1 chicken bouillon cube mixed with 1 cup boiling water

1 cup light cream

2 tablespoons minced fresh flat-leaf parsley

1 Preheat the oven to 350°F. Rub the butter all over the skin of the chicken pieces and season with salt and pepper.

2 In a large ovenproof skillet over medium heat, heat the oil. Cook the chicken, skin side down, for 3 to 5 minutes. Turn over, and cook for 5 minutes longer, or until lightly browned on both sides. Transfer the chicken to a platter. Return the skillet to the heat, stir in the bacon, and cook for 5 to 8 minutes, or until browned. Add the leeks and cook for 3 to 5 minutes, or until soft but not browned. Return the chicken to the pan, season again with salt and pepper, cover with a lid or foil, and bake for 35 to 40 minutes, or until the chicken is no longer pink inside.

3 Remove the skillet from the oven. With a slotted spoon, transfer the chicken, bacon, and leeks to a platter. Return the skillet to medium heat. Stir in the stock or broth and bring to a boil, scraping up all the browned bits from the bottom of the pan with a wooden spoon. Stir in the light cream, reduce the heat to medium-low, and cook for 5 to 7 minutes, or until the mixture thickens slightly.

4 To serve, divide the chicken, bacon, and leeks among 4 plates and spoon the sauce over the top. Sprinkle with the parsley.

• • • • •

A SNUG, THE CROWN LIQUOR SALOON, BELFAST

Flattery's, affectionately known as "Flas," is a family-run pub and restaurant in the picturesque village of Enfield, in County Meath, on the main N4 road from Galway to Dublin. Flattery's has been in the family since 1959, when Martin and Breda Flattery purchased what was then known as Barrington's Hotel. Some locals still refer to it as "the hotel." Flattery's caters to an eclectic mix of people, and is especially known for its interest in and sponsorship of local hurling, rugby, and football clubs. Food is served daily, starting with a carvery lunch, which might include this hearty breast of chicken stuffed with Irish cheese and topped with tomatoes. Serve it with Champ (page 147). Flattery's is a member of Irish Pubs of Distinction (see page 159). **SERVES 4**

Cheese-Stuffed
CHICKEN SUPREME

Four 6-ounce boneless, skinless chicken breast halves

Salt and freshly ground pepper to taste

6 to 8 fresh scallions (white and green parts), minced, with 2 tablespoons reserved for garnish

8 ounces Abbey Brie, or another brie, cut into small pieces

2 tablespoons olive oil

2 tablespoons unsalted Kerrygold Irish butter

1 small onion, diced

8 ounces cherry tomatoes, cut in half, with a few reserved for garnish

2 cups homemade chicken stock (page 60), canned low-sodium chicken broth, or 2 chicken bouillon cubes mixed with 2 cups boiling water

One 8-ounce can tomato purée

6 to 8 fresh basil leaves, chopped, plus 4 whole leaves for garnish

Champ (page 147) for serving

1   Preheat the oven to 375°F. Grease an ovenproof casserole dish.

2   With a sharp knife, cut a pocket in the thick side of each chicken breast half. Season inside and out with salt and pepper. In a small bowl, combine the scallions and cheese, and mash with a fork until well blended. Stuff the cheese mixture into each pocket and press down to close it. Rub the outside of each breast half with olive oil and place in the prepared pan. Bake for 15 minutes, then turn over and bake for 15 minutes more, or until the breasts are no longer pink in the center.

3   Meanwhile, in a medium saucepan over medium heat, melt the butter. Stir in the onion and cook for 3 to 5 minutes, or until soft but not browned. Add the tomatoes and stock or broth and cook for 5 minutes, or until the tomatoes begin to break down. With a fork, remove the tomato skins as they separate from the pulp. Stir in the tomato purée and basil, and bring to a boil. Reduce the heat to medium-low and simmer for 10 to 12 minutes, or until the sauce thickens. Season with salt and pepper.

4   To serve, place a chicken breast in the center of each of 4 plates. Pour some of the sauce over the top and around the chicken breast. Garnish with the reserved scallions and tomatoes, and top with a fresh basil leaf. Serve with Champ.

The village of Strangford, in County Down, snuggles next to Strangford Lough, a natural harbor left by the retreating ice that sculpted the countryside 10,000 years ago. Separating Strangford from Portaferry, the busy lough is crisscrossed hourly by ferries bringing travelers back and forth between north and south County Down. Located in the center of Strangford's village square is the Cuan (meaning "sheltered harbor"), often the first stop for travelers heading in either direction. Visitors enjoy the open fires, cozy bar, and busy restaurant, where chef-proprietor Peter McErlean effortlessly juggles a menu that ranges from the traditional—steak and Guinness pie and sausages and chips—to the exotic. This caramelized duck breast with homemade pineapple chutney comes from the less traditional side of the menu. Prepare the chutney several hours before you plan to serve it and accompany the duck and chutney with the traditional Irish Potato Cakes (page 150), called "boxty." **SERVES 4; MAKES ABOUT 1½ CUPS OF CHUTNEY**

CARAMELIZED DUCK BREAST
with Pineapple Chutney

PINEAPPLE CHUTNEY

2 tablespoons unsalted Kerrygold Irish butter

1 small shallot, minced

1 small pineapple, peeled, quartered, center core removed, and diced; or 1 cup canned pineapple chunks in juice, drained and diced

1 Granny Smith apple, peeled, cored, and diced

1 tablespoon tomato sauce

2 tablespoons light brown sugar

Dash of Irish whiskey

Freshly ground pepper to taste

DUCK

4 boneless duck breast halves, skin on

4 to 5 tablespoons light brown sugar

Potato Cakes (page 150) for serving

CONTINUED

1   **To make the chutney:** In a medium saucepan over medium heat, melt the butter. Cook the shallot for 3 to 5 minutes, or until soft but not browned. Add the pineapple, apple, tomato sauce, and brown sugar. Bring to a boil, then reduce the heat to medium-low and simmer for 15 to 20 minutes, or until the mixture thickens. Stir in the whiskey and season with pepper. Remove from the heat and allow to cool. Refrigerate for up to 24 hours.

2   **To cook the duck:** Preheat the oven to 250°F. Trim the duck breasts and score the skin side. Sprinkle the skin side with the brown sugar and rub in well. In a large ovenproof skillet over medium heat, cook the breasts, skin side down, for 1 minute, then turn and cook for 5 minutes more. The breasts will still be pink inside. Remove the skillet from the heat, turn the breasts, drain, and bake in the oven for 12 to 15 minutes, or until no longer pink in the middle. Remove from the oven and allow to rest for 10 minutes before slicing.

3   To serve, cut each duck breast crosswise into 10 to 12 slices. Place 2 spoonfuls of the pineapple chutney in the center of each of 4 plates and top with duck slices. Serve with the potato cakes.

• • • • •

THE CUAN, STRANGFORD, COUNTY DOWN

At the Ballymore Inn, in Ballymore Eustace, County Kildare, lamb is always popular. In summer, when it's paired with organic herbs and produce grown on local farms, it's unbeatable. Under the direction of the O'Sullivan family, this pub's country kitchen specializes in using traditional, locally sourced ingredients in unusual ways, such as making crispy pizzas with Irish farmhouse cheeses and tossing Irish bacon into a garlicky Caesar salad. To complement this traditional lamb dish, Georgina O'Sullivan pairs it with an aromatic dressing and serves it with a delicious side dish of green beans braised in chicken stock (page 140). Serve this with Mashed Potatoes (page 146). **SERVES 4**

WICKLOW LAMB
with Basil Dressing

BASIL DRESSING

1 bunch (about 2 ounces) fresh basil leaves

1 clove garlic, minced

Juice of 1 lemon

¼ cup extra virgin olive oil

Salt and freshly ground pepper to taste

LAMB

2 racks of lamb, trimmed and cut into
   6 chops each

2 tablespoons balsamic vinegar

Sea salt and freshly ground pepper to taste

2 tablespoons olive oil

1   **To make the dressing:** Combine the basil, garlic, lemon juice, olive oil, salt, and pepper in a food processor or blender, and process until smooth. Set aside.

2   **To cook the lamb:** Lightly rub the chops on both sides with the vinegar and season with salt and pepper. Heat the olive oil in a grill pan or large skillet over medium-high heat, and cook the lamb chops for 3 to 4 minutes on each side, or until done but still pink in the center. Do not overcook. To serve, arrange 3 chops on each of 4 plates and drizzle with the basil dressing. Serve with the green beans and mashed potatoes.

CONTINUED

Braised Green Beans   SERVES 4

2 tablespoons unsalted Kerrygold Irish butter

¼ cup homemade chicken stock (page 60) or canned low-sodium chicken broth

8 ounces fresh green beans, trimmed

Salt and freshly ground pepper to taste

In a large skillet over medium-high heat, melt the butter. Let it brown slightly, then add the chicken stock or broth and bring to a boil. Add the beans, salt, and pepper. Cover, reduce the heat to low, and simmer for 5 to 7 minutes, or until the beans are slightly tender but still crisp.

Pier 36, the pub on the pier at Donaghadee, County Down, has been in the capable hands of the Waterworth family since 1999, when the couple decided to move their inland restaurant business to this new seaside location. An instant success, the busy pub is renowned for its home-style cooking, such as its "roast of the day," a joint of meat slow-roasted in a radiant heat oven known as a Rayburn, or Aga, cooker. This hearty lamb dish served with a red currant glaze is another example. Serve it with Colcannon (page 147). **SERVES 4**

LAMB SHANKS
Glazed with Red Currant Sauce

4 lamb shanks	3 to 4 sprigs fresh thyme
1 leek (white part only), washed and sliced	3 to 4 sprigs fresh rosemary
2 carrots, peeled and sliced	1 cup dry red wine
2 cloves garlic	One 12-ounce jar red currant jelly

1   In a large saucepan or Dutch oven over medium heat, cover the lamb shanks with cold water. Add the leek, carrots, garlic, thyme, and rosemary, and bring to a boil. Reduce the heat to medium-low and simmer for 2 hours, or until the meat is tender when pierced with a fork. Remove from the heat and let cool for at least 1 hour. Cover and refrigerate the lamb in the stock overnight.

2   Preheat the oven to 375°F. Grease an ovenproof baking dish.

3   With a slotted spoon, transfer the shanks to the prepared dish. Bring 2 cups of the stock to a boil. (Discard the rest.) Reduce the heat to medium, and cook for 20 to 30 minutes, or until reduced by half. Stir the wine and red currant jelly into the reduced stock and cook for 10 to 15 minutes, or until the sauce starts to thicken.

4   Spoon half the sauce over the shanks and bake for 15 minutes. Turn over, and bake for 15 minutes longer, or until the lamb is heated through and lightly glazed.

5   To serve, place a lamb shank in the center of each of 4 plates and pour some of the remaining sauce over the top.

Situated in the heart of Belfast, the Garrick Bar on Chichester Street serves one of the finest pub lunches in the city. Its nineteenth-century facade stands out among the undistinguished office buildings that surround it. Once you are inside the pub, its appeal only increases. The Old World décor includes some of Belfast's finest woodwork and tile. The pub is popular with the city's legal crowd since the civil courts are only a few blocks away. A great steak is expected of such an establishment, and it's amply delivered. This stuffed version is spiked with a shot of whiskey. Serve it with Horseradish Mash (page 146). **SERVES 2**

BUSHMILLS STUFFED STEAK

½ cup (1 stick) unsalted Kerrygold Irish butter

1 cup fresh white bread crumbs (see Note, page 33)

Pinch of mixed fresh herbs such as parsley, tarragon, and thyme

Salt and freshly ground pepper to taste

2 tablespoons Bushmills Irish whiskey

Two 6- to 7-ounce boneless rib-eye steaks, butterflied (see Note)

2 tablespoons extra virgin olive oil

1 large shallot, diced

2 to 3 large white mushrooms, quartered

2 to 3 portobello or cremini mushrooms, sliced

1 In a small skillet over medium heat, melt 4 tablespoons of the butter. Stir in the bread crumbs, herbs, and pepper and cook for 2 to 3 minutes, or until the bread crumbs have absorbed the butter. Stir in the whiskey. Season the steak inside and out with salt and pepper. Spread out half the stuffing mixture in the center of each steak, "close" the butterflied steaks, and press down on the meat to seal.

2 In a large skillet over medium-high heat, heat the oil until hot, but not smoking. Cook the steak for 3 to 5 minutes on each side, or until seared. Transfer to a platter, cover with foil, and keep warm.

3 Return the skillet to medium heat, and melt the remaining 4 tablespoons of butter. Add the shallot and mushrooms and cook for 3 to 5 minutes, or until the vegetables are tender. Push them to the side of the pan and return the steaks to the center. Cook for an additional 3 to 5 minutes on each side for medium rare, or until the meat is cooked to your preference and the vegetables are browned.

4 To serve, put a steak in the center of each of 2 plates. Spoon the mushroom mixture and pan juices over the top.

NOTE: *To butterfly the steak, with a sharp knife held parallel to the cutting board, cut horizontally through the steak, peeling back the top as you cut to be sure you're cutting evenly. Stop cutting about ¹/₂ inch before you reach the edge. Flatten out the steak before filling.*

BAILEYS HISTORICAL PUB CRAWL IN BELFAST

No trip to Belfast would be complete without a walk-around to visit its famous and historic pubs. To be sure you don't miss one, Baileys Irish Cream sponsors a two-hour tour led by a professional guide, who provides both history and humor along the way. But don't be put off by the thought of being led around as if you were on a school field trip. There's plenty of time to experience the *craic* (Irish for "good times") in each of the pubs and to enjoy some banter with the locals over a glass of the world's first Irish cream liqueur. There are eleven historic pubs that make up the itinerary, with six visited on a rotating basis.

The tour always begins at the Crown Liquor Saloon, on Great Victoria Street, which boasts one of the most perfectly preserved Victorian pub interiors in all of Ireland (see page 128). Next stop might be the Blackthorn on Skipper Street, a genuine workingman's pub whose clientele ranges from dockworkers and journalists to accountants and warehouse men. Bittles Bar, at Victoria Square, is a curious triangular building decorated with gilded shamrocks and memorabilia celebrating Irish literary figures such as James Joyce, W. B. Yeats, and Oscar Wilde. On Commercial Street, once the heart of the city's newspaper district, the Duke of York is filled with the paraphernalia of the printing trade, with great screw presses and wall murals made entirely of hot metal type. The Garrick, on Chichester Street, is at the heart of the city's commercial district. The pub has been recently restored to reflect its former ambiance in the days when nearby streets were the city's Bohemian quarter (see page 142).

The Kitchen Bar, also at Victoria Square, was once a boardinghouse for young ladies working in a nearby department store. It first opened in 1859 and is noted for its traditional music sessions and hearty lunches. When you step into Maddens, on Berry Street, it's like stepping into the *Gaeltacht* (Irish-speaking area). The small pub hums with the rhythms of Celtic life, and rarely an evening goes by when someone doesn't produce a guitar or fiddle for a music session. McHugh's Bar, at Queen's Square, was originally built more than 300 years ago. As the city's oldest listed building, the pub is often referred to as "the best little alehouse in Belfast." Its restaurant serves both traditional pub food and Asian fare (see page 208). The Morning Star, in Pottingers Entry, is another of the city's oldest pubs. In addition to terrific steaks and chops, the pub also offers more exotic dishes, such as kangaroo and crocodile, thanks to its Australian-born owner. Lastly, White's Tavern, in Winecellar Entry, retains the spirit of a bygone age with an open fire, old world interior, and collection of framed newspaper clippings from the last century. For further details on the Belfast historical pub crawl, see Resources, page 214.

. . . .
THE MORNING STAR, BELFAST

Bangers and mash, steak and mash, pork chops and mash . . . at a meal in Ireland, you're never very far from a side dish of mashed potatoes, whether they're plain, flavored with garlic or horseradish, or mixed with other vegetables, such as cabbage, turnip, or parsnips. Here's the standard recipe for mashed potatoes, along with some variations that pair well with meat, poultry, and seafood. **SERVES 6**

MASHED POTATOES

2¾ to 3 pounds russet potatoes, peeled and cut into 1-inch pieces

1 cup half-and-half

½ cup (1 stick) unsalted Kerrygold Irish butter, cut into pieces

Salt and freshly ground pepper to taste

Cook the potatoes in a large pot of boiling salted water for about 15 minutes, or until tender, and drain. Return them to the same pot to dry out a little. Mash over low heat until almost smooth. Add the half-and-half and butter and whisk until smooth. Season with salt and pepper.

Garlic Mash: Cook the potatoes as described above, drain, and mash until almost smooth. In a small skillet over medium heat, melt ½ cup (1 stick) of unsalted butter. Sauté 1 tablespoon of minced onion and 3 tablespoons of minced garlic for 2 to 3 minutes, or until soft but not browned. Stir the onions and garlic into the potatoes. Stir in 1 cup of half-and-half, mash until smooth over low heat, and season with salt and pepper.

Horseradish Mash: Cook the potatoes, drain, and mash until almost smooth. In a small skillet over medium heat, melt ½ cup (1 stick) of unsalted butter. Stir the butter into the potatoes and add 1 cup of half-and-half and ⅓ cup of prepared horseradish. Season with salt and pepper.

Buttermilk-Chive Mash: Cook the potatoes, drain, and mash until almost smooth. In a small skillet over medium heat, melt $^{1}/_{2}$ cup (1 stick) of unsalted butter. Stir the butter into the potatoes and add 1 cup of buttermilk, $^{1}/_{4}$ cup of half-and-half, $^{1}/_{2}$ teaspoon of dried thyme, and 3 tablespoons of minced fresh chives. Season with salt and pepper.

Crème Fraîche and Dill Mash: Cook the potatoes, drain, and mash until almost smooth. Stir in 4 tablespoons butter, 1 cup of crème fraîche, and 3 tablespoons of minced fresh dill. Season with salt and pepper.

Colcannon: Cook 2 pounds of potatoes, drain, and mash. Cook 1 pound of cabbage, shredded, in boiling salted water for about 15 minutes. Drain, cool slightly, and chop. In a small saucepan over medium heat, combine 1 cup of milk and 2 small leeks, sliced, and cook for 8 to 10 minutes, or until the leeks are tender. Stir the cabbage and leek mixture into the potatoes. Stir in $^{1}/_{2}$ cup (1 stick) of unsalted butter and season with salt and pepper.

Champ: Cook 2 pounds of potatoes, drain, and mash. In a small saucepan over medium heat, combine $^{1}/_{2}$ cup of half-and-half and 6 tablespoons of unsalted butter. Heat until the butter is melted. Stir in $^{1}/_{3}$ cup of minced fresh chives and cook for 2 to 3 minutes, or until the chives are soft. Stir the mixture into the potatoes, and season with salt and pepper.

Jacket potatoes are also popular side dishes for meats. At the Yeats Tavern, a short distance away from W. B. Yeats's burial place at Drumcliff Bridge, County Sligo, Angela Davis bakes the potatoes first, then scoops out the middle, adds ingredients like bacon and cheese, and refills them. The potatoes can be made ahead and reheated at serving time. **SERVES 8**

JACKET POTATOES

4 baking potatoes

4 slices bacon

2 tablespoons fresh minced chives

2 cups crème fraîche (see page 46)

Salt and freshly ground pepper to taste

1 tablespoon minced fresh flat-leaf parsley

4 ounces (1 cup) Cheddar cheese, grated

1   Preheat the oven to 350°F. Bake the potatoes for 35 to 40 minutes, or until tender when pierced with a fork. Remove the potatoes from the oven and let cool for 5 to 10 minutes. Maintain oven temperature.

2   Meanwhile, in a large skillet, cook the bacon until crisp. Transfer to paper towels to drain. When cool, crumble into bits.

3   Cut the potatoes in half lengthwise. Scoop out the flesh into a medium bowl. Stir in the bacon, chives, crème frâiche, salt, pepper, parsley, and cheese. Refill each potato half with the mixture. Transfer the potatoes to a baking sheet and bake for 15 to 20 minutes, or until the mixture is heated through.

4   Preheat the broiler. Move the baking sheet to 4 inches from the heat source, and broil for 1 to 2 minutes, or until the tops of the potatoes are lightly browned. Serve immediately.

• • • • •
COUNTY WICKLOW COUNTRYSIDE

Potato cakes, griddle cakes, and chips (the equivalent of French fries) are popular alternatives to mashed potatoes. Some potato cakes, like these, which are known as boxty, are made with a combination of mashed and raw potatoes. **MAKES ABOUT 16 POTATO CAKES**

POTATO CAKES

1 pound boiling potatoes, peeled

1 cup Mashed Potatoes (page 146)

2 tablespoons all-purpose flour

½ cup milk

1 teaspoon baking powder

1 teaspoon salt

¼ cup canola oil

1 Line a large bowl with a piece of muslin or cheesecloth or a clean linen towel. Using the large holes of a box grater, grate the boiling potatoes into the bowl. Squeeze the cloth to extract as much of the starchy liquid as possible. Discard the liquid, return the potatoes to the bowl, and stir in the mashed potatoes, flour, milk, baking powder, and salt.

2 Preheat the oven to 200°F. In a large skillet over medium heat, warm the oil. Drop the potato mixture, 1 tablespoonful at a time, into the skillet; do not crowd the pan. Flatten each cake with a spatula and cook for 3 to 4 minutes on each side, or until lightly browned and crisp. Transfer the cakes to a baking sheet and keep warm. Repeat until you have used up all the potato mixture, adding more oil as necessary.

Crisp Potato Cakes   MAKES ABOUT 8 POTATO CAKES

Grate 1 pound of potatoes as described above. Stir in ¹/₂ cup of minced fresh chives, salt, and pepper. Shape the mixture into cakes 2 inches in diameter. Fry the cakes as described above, until browned and crisp. Drain on paper towels.

Rösti   SERVES 4 TO 6

Cook 1 pound of whole boiling potatoes, unpeeled, in a large pot of boiling salted water for about 25 minutes, or until tender. Drain and cool. Refrigerate the potatoes, covered, for about 2 hours. Peel the potatoes, and using the large holes of a box grater, shred into a bowl. Season with salt and pepper. In a large nonstick skillet over medium heat, melt 1 tablespoon of unsalted butter with 1¹/₂ teaspoons of olive oil. Add the potatoes and spread to form a large cake. Reduce the heat to low and cook for 10 to 12 minutes, or until the bottom of the rösti is lightly browned and crisp. Run a spatula around the edges, slide onto a large plate, and invert onto another plate. Melt 1 tablespoon of unsalted butter in the skillet and slide the rösti back into the pan, uncooked side down. Cook for 10 to 12 minutes, or until the bottom is browned and crisp. Slide the rösti onto a serving plate and cut into wedges.

Cider makers often develop recipes for restaurants and pubs to promote their product. This comes from Bulmers, Ireland's leading brand of cider. The company traces its origins to 1935, when William Magner started to ferment hard cider in Clonmel, County Tipperary. Cider has long been a popular ingredient in many European cuisines, particularly among the Celts, Bretons, and Normans. Irish chefs love to use it, too, often as a substitute for wine, because of the unique flavor it imparts to sauces, meat, and poultry. This chicken dish is cooked coq au vin–style in Magners, a dry cider with a lively, crisp taste. Serve this with Mashed Potatoes (page 146). **SERVES 6**

BLACKBOARD SPECIAL

Cider-Braised
CHICKEN AND CABBAGE

⅓ cup all-purpose flour

Salt and freshly ground pepper to taste

Six 5- to 6-ounce bone-in chicken breast halves, skin on

¼ cup olive oil

4 to 5 cloves garlic

3 carrots, peeled and thickly sliced

1 large onion, thickly sliced

3 bay leaves

½ cup golden raisins

2 tablespoons minced fresh flat-leaf parsley

2 tablespoons fresh rosemary

2 cups shredded Savoy cabbage

1 cup homemade chicken stock (page 60), canned low-sodium chicken broth, or 1 chicken bouillon cube mixed with 1 cup boiling water

1 cup Irish cider, preferably Magners brand

1 Preheat the oven to 325°F. Combine the flour, salt, and pepper in a shallow bowl and dredge the chicken in it, shaking off the excess.

2 In a large skillet over medium heat, warm the oil. Add the chicken in batches and cook for 3 to 4 minutes on each side, or until lightly browned. Transfer the chicken to a large ovenproof baking dish.

3 Tuck the garlic, carrots, onions, and bay leaves in between the chicken pieces. Sprinkle with the raisins, parsley, and rosemary. Place the cabbage on top, season with salt and pepper, and pour the stock or broth and cider over the meat and vegetables. Cover with foil and bake for 1¼ to 1½ hours, or until the chicken is tender.

4 To serve, place a chicken breast in the center of each of 6 plates, and spoon the vegetables and sauce over the top.

CHAPTER 6

SEAFOOD

Ireland is blessed with hundreds of miles of coastline, thousands of miles of sparkling rivers, and acres of pristine lakes, called "loughs" in Ireland. Dublin prawns, Galway oysters, Bantry mussels, and Kenmare scallops are famous in the Republic. In Ulster, their counterparts hail from places like Portavogie, Carlingford, Ardlass, and Murlough Bay. Herrings from Sligo and brown trout from Lough Corrib are nearly legendary, and Lough Neigh eels were rated "the fairest and the fattest" by a seventeenth-century archbishop. Simplicity is the key to Irish seafood cookery, and freshness is guaranteed by pub chefs, who rely on the catch of the day from local waters.

•••••
BLACKBOARD SPECIAL, GALWAY CITY

Durty Nelly's, also known as the Village Inn, was established in 1620 in Bunratty, County Clare. It's one of the most popular attractions in the area for visitors and locals alike, with three bars, two restaurants, and a pleasant picnic area in front. It is named for a local woman who was keeper of the toll bridge that once was adjacent to the inn, and her history is indeed a lively one (see page 86). One of the pub's most popular recipes is this easy-to-prepare monkfish, which comes wrapped in bacon and topped with mustard dressing. Serve this with Garlic Mash (page 146), if you wish. SERVES 4

ROASTED MONKFISH
Wrapped in Bacon with Mustard Dressing

MUSTARD DRESSING

1 tablespoon whole-grain mustard

½ teaspoon Dijon mustard

1 tablespoon superfine sugar

1 tablespoon soy sauce

1 tablespoon rice wine vinegar

3 tablespoons canola oil

Four 5- to 6-ounce pieces monkfish

8 streaky rashers (traditional Irish bacon; see page 53)

2 tablespoons canola oil

1   **To make the dressing:** Combine the mustards, sugar, soy sauce, and vinegar in a small bowl and whisk until the sugar is dissolved. Add the oil, whisking until well blended.

2   Preheat the oven to 350°F. Grease an ovenproof casserole dish.

3   Wrap each piece of monkfish with 2 rashers. In a large skillet over medium heat, warm the oil. Cook the fish on all sides to seal (about 2 to 3 minutes total). Transfer to the prepared dish and roast for 10 minutes, or until the bacon is cooked through.

4   To serve, put 1 piece of monkfish in the center of each of 4 plates and drizzle with the mustard dressing.

IRISH PUBS OF DISTINCTION

Much of Ireland's social life revolves around the pub, from traditional ones with open-hearth fires and flagstone flooring to stylishly modern ones filled with chrome and glass. No matter what the style, the pub is where old friends meet new ones, where computer geeks and farmers alike go to unwind after a busy day of work, and where you're most likely to find an impromptu music session ready to get underway.

Irish Pubs of Distinction is a group of independently owned and operated pubs that offers a kind of quality assurance, which is especially helpful for visitors looking for pubs with warm hospitality and good service and food. Most of the pubs in the group, which is an initiative of the Vintners' Federation of Ireland, pride themselves on the food they serve, and some even offer breakfast and sleeping accommodations. The stated mission of the members is to ensure that your Irish pub experience will "linger in your heart and soul for a long time to come." There are currently seventy-four member pubs in twenty-two counties, many of which have offered recipes for this cookbook. To locate a member, see Resources, page 214.

The Fiddle [ ] the Square in the historic town of Portaferry, in County Down, is almost as well known [ ] as it is for its food, much of which has distinctive overtones of the Far East. Traditional [ ] ckseat, however. Chef Chris Wellington is always anxious to utilize the fresh seafood c [ ] around the Ards Peninsula and Strangford Lough, where Portaferry is located. T[ ]med for its atmospheric bar, as well as for its maritime-themed Quarterdeck Restaurar [ ] luces traditional Irish dishes that combine the best ingredients from farm and sea. [ ] flavored risotto, paired with local salmon, is a good example. **SERVES 4**

PAN-SEARED SALMON
with Basil Risotto

RISOTTO

2 cups homemade fish stock (page 62) or bottled clam juice, or 2 fish bouillon cubes mixed with 2 cups boiling water

1 cup dry white wine

2 tablespoons unsalted Kerrygold Irish butter

1 tablespoon olive oil

2 tablespoons minced onion

1 tablespoon minced garlic

1½ cups Arborio rice

¼ cup grated Parmesan cheese

Salt and freshly ground pepper to taste

2 tablespoons minced fresh basil

SALMON

2 tablespoons olive oil, plus additional for drizzling

Four 5- to 6-ounce salmon fillets

1 tablespoon unsalted Kerrygold Irish butter

4 ounces rocket (arugula) for garnish

1 **To make the risotto:** In a medium saucepan over medium heat, combine the fish stock or clam juice and wine. Bring to a simmer and keep warm.

2 In a large skillet over medium heat, melt the butter with the olive oil. Add the onion and garlic and cook for 2 to 3 minutes, or until soft but not browned. Add the rice and stir until coated. Add 1 cup of the simmering stock mixture and cook, stirring constantly, until the stock is absorbed. Continue cooking in this way, adding the stock mixture, about $^1/_2$ cup at a time, and stirring constantly to prevent the rice from sticking, until all the stock has been used, about 20 to 25 minutes. Stir in the cheese and season with salt and pepper. Sprinkle with the basil and keep warm.

3 **To cook the salmon:** In a large skillet over medium heat, warm the olive oil. Add the salmon, skin side down, and cook for 2 to 4 minutes, or until seared. Turn over, add the butter, and cook for 8 to 10 minutes more, or until no longer opaque.

4 To serve, divide the risotto among 4 shallow bowls and put a salmon fillet on top of each serving. Garnish with rocket (arugula) and drizzle with a little of the additional olive oil.

The Me[...] [...]staurant situated in the idyllic Vale of Avoca, also known as "The Meeting of the Wa[...] [...] where the Avonmore and Avonbeag rivers meet. It's a popular destination for the [...] [...]cenic area of County Wicklow. Lovers of Irish poetry often visit to honor Thoma[...] [...]onal poet who immortalized the area in a poem that takes as its title the poetic [...] [...]tion. The pub pays homage to him in a lovely mural, complete with a few verse[...] [...]ry and scenery aside, food at the Meetings is wholesome and hearty. Local seafood, like this stuffed salmon, is featured daily. Serve it with Spinach-Chive Sauce (page 164) and Buttermilk-Chive Mash (page 147). The Meetings is a member of Irish Pubs of Distinction (see page 159). SERVES 4

STUFFED SALMON EN CROÛTE

½ cup (1 stick) unsalted Kerrygold Irish butter

1 small onion, diced

½ cup fresh white bread crumbs (see Note, page 33)

Zest and juice of 1 lemon

Zest and juice of 1 lime

2 teaspoons fresh tarragon

1 teaspoon ground coriander

2 sheets frozen puff pastry from a 17.3-ounce package, left at room temperature for 30 minutes

Four 5- to 6-ounce salmon fillets, skin removed

1 large egg beaten with 1 tablespoon water

Spinach-Chive Sauce (page 164) for serving

1   Preheat the oven to 400°F. Grease a baking sheet.

2   In a medium skillet over medium heat, melt the butter. Add the onion and cook for 3 to 5 minutes, or until soft but not browned. Remove the pan from the heat and stir in the bread crumbs, zest and juice of the lemon and lime, the tarragon, and coriander. Mix well and set aside.

CONTINUED

3   Unfold the pastry sheets on a lightly floured surface. Roll out each into a 12-inch square, and cut it in half. Place a salmon fillet on one half of each of the rectangles of pastry, leaving a 1-inch border. Spoon some of the stuffing mix on top of each piece of salmon and with your fingers, press down firmly to cover the fish. Brush the borders of the pastry with egg wash—1 inch on the salmon half, and 1 1/2 inches on the other half—and fold over to make a parcel. Press the edges of the pastry together with a fork to seal, and prick the top to allow for steam to escape. Brush with the egg wash.

4   Place the salmon parcels on the prepared baking sheet and bake for 30 to 35 minutes, or until the pastry is golden.

5   To serve, place a salmon parcel in the center of each of 4 plates and spoon some of the Spinach-Chive Sauce around it.

Spinach-Chive Sauce   MAKES ABOUT 1¾ CUPS

½ cup heavy (whipping) cream	6 ounces spinach, washed and trimmed
4 tablespoons unsalted Kerrygold Irish butter	1 tablespoon olive oil
½ cup minced shallots	¼ teaspoon salt
1½ cups chopped fresh chives	¼ teaspoon white pepper

1   In a small saucepan over medium heat, bring the cream to a boil. Reduce the heat to medium, and cook gently for 4 to 5 minutes, or until reduced by half.

2   In a large skillet over medium heat, melt 2 tablespoons of the butter. Cook the shallots for 3 to 4 minutes, or until soft but not browned. Add the chives and spinach, cover, and cook, stirring occasionally, for 2 to 3 minutes, or until the spinach is wilted. Transfer the mixture to a food processor or blender, add the reduced cream, the remaining 2 tablespoons of butter, the oil, salt, and pepper. Process for 10 to 15 seconds, or until smooth. Cover and refrigerate for up to 24 hours.

...illage of Tarmonbarry sits on the banks of the river Shannon in County Roscommon. A genuine ...f interest in the village is Keenan's, a pub established in the late 1860s and still operated by the ...family. While the pub has changed over the years and each generation has developed its own ...continues to upgrade its menu to keep pace with current trends. With great fishing and boating ...hannon, it's no surprise to find many fish dishes served there, such as this flavorful casserole ...h smoked haddock. The chef suggests you serve it spooned over Mashed Potatoes or Champ. ...is a member of Irish Pubs of Distinction (see page 159). **SERVES 4**

SMOKED HADDOCK CASSEROLE

1 tablespoon canola oil
8 ounces white mushrooms, sliced
1 large onion, diced
⅔ cup light cream
⅔ cup milk
1½ pounds smoked haddock, cut into ½-inch
  pieces

1 tablespoon freshly ground pepper
1 small tomato, finely chopped
Mashed Potatoes or Champ (page 146 or 147)
  for serving
2 tablespoons minced fresh flat-leaf parsley
  for garnish

1   In a large skillet over medium heat, warm the oil. Add the mushrooms and onions and cook for
    3 to 4 minutes, or until soft but not browned. Add the cream, lower the heat, and simmer for 5 to
    7 minutes, or until reduced by half. Set aside.

2   In a small saucepan over medium heat, gently bring the milk to a boil. Add the smoked haddock
    and cook for 4 to 5 minutes, or until lightly poached. Season with pepper.

3   Add the poached haddock mixture to the mushroom mixture, gently bring to a boil, then lower
    the heat and simmer for 8 to 10 minutes, or until thickened. Add the chopped tomato and cook for
    1 minute to heat through.

4   To serve, put a few spoonfuls of the potatoes in the center of each of 4 plates and spoon the smoked
    haddock around it. Sprinkle with the parsley.

LITERARY AND MUSICAL
PUB CRAWLS IN DUBLIN

Some of Ireland's greatest writers and poets lived, worked, and drank in Dublin, so it's no surprise to find a pub crawl there that lets you follow in the footsteps of literary giants by visiting their favorite watering holes. During an animated and entertaining walking tour, you get a crash course in Irish literature, history, architecture, and street theater as you visit five or six pubs with ties to writers such as James Joyce, Sean O'Casey, Samuel Beckett, Oscar Wilde, and Brendan Behan.

The guides are two professional actors who perform extracts from famous literary works—some serious, some coarse and bawdy, some tongue-in-cheek—and tell stories about the personal lives of the authors. During the tourist season, two tours take place nightly, beginning at the Duke, a pub on Duke Street associated with James Joyce. In most cases, the tours are filled with an international group of tourists who, as one German told me, like the idea of "directed drinking" as opposed to "reckless rambling." There is a stop at Trinity College, where an excerpt from an Oscar Wilde work is usually performed, and at the Dublin Tourist Center, an old Viking site. Then the crawl visits O'Neill's Pub on Suffolk Street and the Old Stand on Exchequer Street, and finishes again on Duke Street at Davy Byrnes, the "moral pub" mentioned in Joyce's *Ulysses*. The tour generally lasts between two to two-and-a-half hours, depending, as the guide reminds, "on how slowly you walk and how quickly you drink."

If Irish music is more to your liking, there's also a musical pub crawl around the Temple Bar area of the city that's another great way to enjoy Dublin's lively pub scene. Two professional musicians lead this one. They play a little and drink a little, in between telling you about the history of Irish music, the various instruments that make up this traditional musical genre, and its influence on contemporary world music. The tour meets in Oliver St. John Gogarty's pub on Fleet Street and visits pubs such as Ha'penny Bridge Inn, the Palace Bar, Isolde's Tower, the Chancery, and the Legal Eagle. The two-and-a-half-hour crawl takes place nightly from May to October and on weekends during other times of the year. For further details on the Dublin pub crawls, see Resources, page 214.

. . . .

FARRINGTON'S OF TEMPLE BAR, DUBLIN

Kilmore Quay is a rural fishing village in County Wexford, situated in the sunny southeast corner of Ireland. One of the village's most distinctive features is the number of thatched cottages that line its streets, most of which date to the eighteenth and nineteenth centuries. Kehoe's Pub and Parlour, one of Kilmore Quay's most popular spots, enjoys the unique distinction of having been in the Kehoe family for six generations; until 1987 it was the family home, where several generations were reared. Complete with a maritime heritage center on the premises, the pub is known for its famous seafood kitchen. Specialties like stuffed baked cod, ocean pie, and this seafood mornay top their menu. Serve this dish with Buttermilk-Chive Mash (page 147), if you wish. **SERVES 4**

SEAFOOD MORNAY

1 pound cod

8 ounces smoked haddock

6 ounces salmon fillet

SAUCE

Homemade fish stock (page 62) or bottled clam juice, as needed

4 cups milk

1 cup dry white wine

2 tablespoons cornstarch

10 ounces Kerrygold Vintage Cheddar cheese or another aged Cheddar, grated

2 tablespoons Dijon mustard

Salt and ground white pepper to taste

1   Preheat the oven to 400°F. Butter 4 individual gratin dishes.

2   **To cook the fish:** In a medium skillet over medium heat, combine the cod and smoked haddock. Add cold water to cover, bring to a simmer, and poach for 10 minutes, or until no longer opaque. In a separate medium skillet over medium heat, add enough water to cover the salmon, bring to a simmer, and poach it for 10 minutes, or until no longer opaque. Strain the fish and reserve the poaching liquids. Combine the fish in a large bowl, flake with a fork, and divide among the prepared dishes.

3   **To make the sauce:** In a medium saucepan over medium heat, combine the reserved poaching liquids and add enough fish stock or clam juice to measure 4 cups. Add 3¾ cups of the milk and the wine and bring to a boil. In a small bowl, whisk together the remaining ¼ cup of milk and the cornstarch to make a roux. Stir into the sauce, reduce the heat to medium-low, and simmer, stirring constantly, for 4 to 6 minutes, or until the sauce starts to thicken. Stir in half the cheese, the mustard, and season with salt and pepper. Spoon the sauce over the fish and sprinkle with the remaining half of the cheese. Bake for 15 to 18 minutes, or until the tops are brown and the sauce is bubbling.

Northern Ireland's Kingdoms of Down offer a unique palette of spectacular scenery ranging from miles of pretty coastline to the famous Mountains of Mourne that run down to the sea. The Strangford Lough area, on the northeast coast, is especially beautiful, with quaint and picturesque towns dotting both sides of the Ards Peninsula, from Newtownards to Portaferry. At Kircubbin, on the west coast of the Ards, Finnegan's Pub has been licensed for more than fifty years, after being converted from a nineteenth-century coaching house. Appearances can be deceiving, so once you get over the rough-around-the-edges interior furnishings, you'll be impressed with the confident, simple, and beautifully unfussy approach to their food, especially their seafood. This prawn and bacon dish is delicious accompanied with a Potato Cake or boiled new potatoes. **SERVES 4**

PRAWNS AND BACON
with Mustard Sauce

MUSTARD SAUCE

1 cup homemade fish stock (page 62), bottled clam juice, or 1 fish bouillon cube mixed with 1 cup boiling water

¾ cup heavy (whipping) cream

2 teaspoons English-style mustard, preferably Coleman's

1 tablespoon minced fresh flat-leaf parsley

Salt and freshly ground pepper

4 streaky rashers (traditional Irish bacon; see page 53), cut into thin strips

1 tablespoon sunflower oil

1 pound prawns (jumbo shrimp), peeled and deveined

Lemon wedges for garnish

Dill sprigs for garnish

Potato Cakes (page 150) or boiled new potatoes for serving

1   **To make the mustard sauce:** In a small saucepan over medium heat, bring the fish stock or clam juice to a boil. Cook for 8 to 10 minutes, or until reduced by half. Whisk in $^1/_2$ cup of the cream and cook for 5 to 8 minutes, or until the sauce starts to thicken. Whisk in the mustard, the remaining $^1/_4$ cup of cream, and the parsley. Cook for 5 to 7 minutes, or until smooth. Season with salt and pepper. Keep warm over low heat.

2   In a large dry skillet over medium heat, cook the bacon for 5 to 7 minutes, or until crisp. Set aside.

3   In a large clean skillet, heat the oil over medium-high heat until nearly smoking. Stir in the prawns and cook for 2 minutes on each side, or until they turn pink and are lightly browned. Stir in the reserved bacon and cook for 30 seconds, or until heated through.

4   To serve, place the prawns on a hot serving plate and spoon the mustard sauce over them. Garnish with lemon wedges and fresh dill, and serve with potatoes.

THE SHOP FRONTS OF IRELAND

One of the most distinctive features of an Irish pub is the traditional design and architecture of its facade. Many towns and villages have become world famous for the quality, design, and craftsmanship of their shop fronts. They come in a variety of shapes, designs, and colors, from the highly decorative Greek Revival ones, with an entablature resting on pilasters or columns, to the plain styles found on many small country shops and pubs. The windows and door are generally placed in pleasing proportion to one another.

Some of the earliest shop fronts, particularly those that date from the eighteenth century, have small panes of glass set vertically in small bow windows, while others have leaded fanlights over the doors. In the mid-nineteenth century, two-by four-inch glass panes were introduced, which encouraged perpendicular shop front designs. These have heavy, round-headed mullions (vertical divisions between the panes), sometimes with tiny capitals and carved panels in the triangular pediments above them. Large panes of plate glass, filling the entire window, were not introduced until late in the nineteenth century.

Shop names were painted on fascia boards or raised letters were carved into them. During the late nineteenth century, several attractive forms of lettering were introduced, including raised marbled ceramic, and channeled letter or trompe l'oeil, both of which gave an artificial three-dimensional effect and were often placed behind glass. Most shop fronts are painted in strong colors, which are slow to fade, and many are given an added decorative touch with graining, staining, and marbling wood and plaster.

Pub signs are another interesting aspect of Irish pub design. Cian Molloy, author of *The Story of the Irish Pub,* tells us that "in the late nineteenth century, the Irish abandoned the English-style pub sign with names like 'The Nag's Head' or 'The Crown'—illustrated as an aid to those who couldn't read—and chose instead to adopt the practice of naming the pub after the current licensee or the family name of the pub's founder." This remains a common practice.

Originally known as the Kings Arms, a pub that first opened in 1611, Grace Neill's, on High Street in Donaghadee, County Down, is currently under the direction of chef-proprietor Neil Savage. He has transformed one of Ireland's oldest pubs into one of its hottest dining destinations (see pages 86–87) with an antique front bar, stylish library bar, and contemporary restaurant. His version of traditional fish 'n' chips (adapted here) is prepared with a lighter-than-air beer batter and served with a jaunty lemon aioli sauce instead of the traditional malt vinegar. **SERVES 4**

COD 'N' CHIPS
with Lemon Aioli

LEMON AIOLI
½ cup mayonnaise
2 tablespoons fresh lemon juice
1½ teaspoons grated lemon zest
1½ teaspoons Dijon mustard
1 teaspoon red wine vinegar
¼ cup olive oil
Salt and freshly ground pepper to taste

CHIPS
2½ pounds russet potatoes
Canola oil for frying

BATTER
2 cups self-rising flour
1 teaspoon baking soda
½ teaspoon salt
1 teaspoon ground white pepper
1 cup ice water
1 teaspoon white wine vinegar
½ cup cold Irish ale, such as Smithwick's
2 teaspoons grated fresh ginger

2 pounds cod fillets
Salt and freshly ground pepper to taste

To make the aioli: In a small bowl, combine the mayonnaise, lemon juice, lemon zest, mustard, and vinegar. Whisk in the oil until smooth. Season with salt and pepper. Cover and refrigerate for up to 24 hours.

CONTINUED

2 **To make the chips:** Preheat the oven to 250°F. Line 2 baking pans with paper towels. Peel the potatoes, cut them into $^1/_2$-inch-thick wedges, then transfer to a large bowl of cold water. Pour enough
oil into a large heavy pot to reach a depth of 3 inches, or fill an electric deep fryer three quarters
full with oil. Heat until a deep-fat thermometer registers 300°F. Drain the potatoes and dry with
paper towels. Working in batches, add the potatoes to the oil and cook, stirring occasionally, for
3 to 4 minutes per batch, or until the potatoes are just tender. With a slotted spoon, transfer to one
of the prepared baking sheets to drain. Heat the same oil to 350°F. Working in batches again, refry
the potatoes for 2 minutes per batch, or until golden brown. Transfer to the second baking sheet
to drain. Sprinkle with salt and keep warm in the oven. Increase the oil temperature to 375°F.

3 **To make the batter:** In a large bowl, sift together the flour, baking soda, salt, and pepper. Stir in
the water, vinegar, beer, and grated ginger to form a batter. Do not overwork it.

4 **To cook the fish:** Coat 2 to 3 pieces of cod with the batter and slide into the oil. Fry the fish, turning
frequently, for 4 to 5 minutes, or until golden. Transfer to a paper towel–lined baking sheet to drain,
then keep warm in the oven. Fry the remaining fish in batches, returning the oil to 375°F each time.
Season the cod and chips with salt and pepper and serve immediately with the Lemon Aioli.

• • • • •
PATRON ENJOYING A PINT AT GRACE NEILL'S LIBRARY BAR, DONAGHADEE, COUNTY DOWN

"IF ALL BE TRUE THAT I DO THINK
THERE ARE FIVE REASONS WE
GOOD WINE - A FRIEND - OR
OR LEST
BE BY
OR

One of County Galway's best-known pubs, Paddy Burkes Oyster Inn, in Clarenbridge, is frequently associated with the oyster festival held in the village each September (see page 17). Since it's located only a stone's throw from some of the country's best seafood and shellfish beds, you can be sure to find a wide selection on the menu there. This bountiful mélange of freshly harvested seafood, which arrives bubbling in a colorful herb-topped sauce, is a delicious example. SERVES 2

(see page 17)

◇═══════════ ● BLACKBOARD SPECIAL ● ═══════════◇

Paddy Burkes
HARVEST OF THE SEA

◇══════════════════════════════════════◇

2 ounces fresh salmon, cut into 2-inch pieces

2 ounces cod, cut into 2-inch pieces

2 ounces monkfish, cut into 2-inch pieces

4 prawns (jumbo shrimp), unshelled

2 scallops, cut in half

2 oysters, scrubbed

6 mussels, scrubbed and debearded

¼ cup dry white wine

¼ cup fresh lemon juice

1 tablespoon minced fresh flat-leaf parsley

FISH VELOUTÉ SAUCE

2 tablespoons unsalted Kerrygold Irish butter

3 tablespoons all-purpose flour

Salt and pepper to taste

1 cup homemade fish stock (page 62), or bottled clam juice, or 1 fish bouillon cube mixed with 1 cup boiling water

⅓ cup half-and-half

¼ cup heavy (whipping) cream

2 teaspoons minced fresh dill

1 teaspoon minced fresh tarragon

1 teaspoon minced fresh chives

Lemon wedges for garnish

1 Preheat the oven to 350°F. Butter an ovenproof casserole dish.

2 Put all the fish and shellfish in the prepared dish and pour the wine and lemon juice over them. Sprinkle with parsley. Cover with wax paper and then aluminum foil. Bake for 20 to 30 minutes, or until the fish are cooked and the oysters and mussels have opened. Discard any that do not open.

CONTINUED

3   While the seafood cooks, make the fish velouté sauce: In a small saucepan over medium heat, melt the butter. Whisk in the flour until smooth. Season with salt and pepper. Whisk in the fish stock or clam juice, bring to a boil, and cook for 2 minutes, or until it starts to thicken. Stir in the half-and-half and cook for 2 minutes more, or until smooth. Keep warm over low heat.

4   Preheat the broiler.

5   Drain the poaching liquid from the cooked seafood into a small saucepan and place over medium heat. (Keep the fish covered.) Cook for 5 to 8 minutes, or until reduced by half. Stir in the fish velouté sauce and cream and cook for 5 minutes, or until the sauce thickens.

6   Arrange the fish and shellfish on a shallow, heat-proof serving dish and spoon the sauce over the seafood. Put the dish under the broiler, 4 inches from the heat source, and broil for 45 to 60 seconds, or until the sauce is lightly browned and bubbling. Remove from the broiler, sprinkle with dill, tarragon, and chives and garnish with lemon wedges.

PADDY BURKES OYSTER INN, CLARENBRIDGE, COUNTY GALWAY

CHAPTER 7

SWEETS

All Irish people have a sweet tooth, so whether you're visiting someone's home, meeting for tea in a restaurant, or dropping into your local pub, you can be certain something sweet will be on the menu. A simple tart, a piece of cake, or a warm pudding is a sure bet, although more ambitious kitchens might also offer a decadent chocolate concoction or a boozy cheesecake. Many sweets are served with a small pot of freshly whipped cream.

The O'Crowley family, proprietors of An Súgán, in Clonakilty, County Cork, love to serve Pavlova, a popular Irish dessert named for a Russian ballerina. Sometimes called "meringue nests," the dessert consists of a crisp meringue base topped with whipped cream and fresh fruit, especially local strawberries or raspberries when they're in season. **SERVES 6**

PAVLOVA
with Fresh Fruit

MERINGUES
4 large egg whites
Pinch of salt
1¼ cups superfine sugar
2 teaspoons cornstarch
1 teaspoon distilled white vinegar

FILLING
2 cups heavy (whipping) cream
1 teaspoon superfine sugar
1 pint strawberries, hulled and sliced
1 pint raspberries

1 **To make the meringues:** Preheat the oven to 250°F. Line a baking sheet with parchment paper.

2 For uniform nests, draw six 4-inch circles on the paper. Turn the paper over, and secure with masking tape. In a medium bowl, combine the egg whites and salt. With an electric mixer, beat on low speed for 4 to 5 minutes, or until soft peaks form, them increase the speed to high and gradually beat in the sugar. Continue to beat until stiff peaks form. Beat in the cornstarch and vinegar.

3 Transfer the mixture to a pastry bag fitted with a ¹/₂-inch star tip, and pipe it to fill the rounds you drew on the parchment paper. Or spoon the mixture into mounds. Depress the center with a spoon to create a "nest." Bake for 1¹/₂ to 2 hours, or until the meringues are crisp. Turn off the oven and let them cool completely inside. When cooled, slide a spatula or knife between them and the paper to separate. (The meringues can be stored in an airtight container for up to 1 week.)

4 **To fill the meringues:** In a medium bowl, combine the cream and sugar and beat with an electric mixer until stiff peaks form. Divide the strawberries and raspberries among the meringues and top with the whipped cream.

CONTINUED

Pavlova with Lemon Curd

Prepare the meringues as described above. Fill with prepared lemon curd and top with fresh berries and whipped cream.

Cocoa Meringues

In a medium bowl, beat the egg whites with an electric mixer on low for 4 to 5 minutes, or until soft peaks form. Add a pinch of cream of tartar, increase the speed to high, and gradually beat in $1/2$ cup of sugar. Continue to beat until stiff peaks form. Sift 2 teaspoons of cocoa powder and $1/2$ teaspoon of cinnamon over the egg whites and fold in gently. Bake as described in the recipe above. Fill the meringues with vanilla ice cream and top with chocolate or hot fudge sauce.

Situated in Kilkenny, one of the loveliest medieval cities in Ireland, Kyteler's Inn is a tavern that dates from 1324. It's the favorite haunt of locals and visitors alike, many of whom are intrigued by the legend of Dame Alice Le Kyteler, the original owner (see pages 86–87). Full of character and charm, folklore and history, the tavern has cut stone walls, oak beams, stripped timbered floors, wooden tables, and open fires that add to its ambiance. Atmosphere aside, the emphasis is always on homemade food with both traditional Irish and European influences. This Irish cream cheesecake is considered a house specialty. **SERVES 10 TO 12**

IRISH CREAM CHEESECAKE

CRUST

1 cup crumbs from Irish digestive biscuits or wheat biscuits, such as Carr's or McVitie's brand (6 to 8 biscuits)

3 tablespoons sugar

3 tablespoons unsalted Kerrygold Irish butter, melted

FILLING

1 cup heavy (whipping) cream

4 large eggs, separated

One ¼-ounce envelope unflavored gelatin

¾ cup boiling water

½ cup sugar

One 8-ounce package cream cheese at room temperature

¾ cup Baileys Irish Cream liqueur

1 **To make the crust:** Preheat the oven to 350°F. In a small bowl, combine the crumbs, sugar, and melted butter. Press the crumb mixture onto the bottom and up the sides of a 9-inch round spring-form pan. Bake for 8 to 10 minutes, or until lightly browned. Remove from the oven and let cool on a wire rack.

2 **To make the filling:** Whip the cream in a medium bowl with an electric mixer until soft peaks form. With clean beaters, in another medium bowl, whip the egg whites with an electric mixer until stiff peaks form. Gently fold the egg whites into the whipped cream.

3 In a small bowl, combine the gelatin and boiling water. Stir until the gelatin is completely dissolved, about 5 minutes. In a large bowl, combine the sugar and egg yolks, and beat with an electric mixer for 4 to 5 minutes, or until light and fluffy. Beat in the cream cheese and Baileys until smooth. Stir in the gelatin and the whipped cream mixture. Pour over the biscuit crust and refrigerate for 3 to 4 hours, or until firm.

4 When ready to serve, release the sides of the pan and cut the cheesecake into wedges.

The White House, in Kinsale, County Cork, is one of the town's oldest licensed establishments. A landmark for generations, the bar is handsomely designed with a pine floor, warm yellow walls, beamed rafters, globe lighting, and plenty of comfortable tartan-covered seating. Under the direction of the Frawley family for more than 140 years, the White House is also a busy hotel. It has a modern bar in addition to the pub, bistro, and Restaurant D'Antibes, where chef Mark Russell is in charge of the kitchen. His inventive cheesecake is flavored with Murphy's, the famous Cork-brewed stout. It is served in both the restaurant and pub and is a long-standing favorite. **SERVES 10 TO 12**

MURPHY'S AND BAILEYS CHEESECAKE

CRUMB CRUST

1 cup crumbs from gingersnaps or Irish digestive biscuits, such as Carr's or McVitie's brand (6 to 8 biscuits)

3 tablespoons unsalted Kerrygold Irish butter, melted

SYRUP

4 cups Murphy's stout

2 cups dark brown sugar

FILLING

One 8-ounce package cream cheese at room temperature

1 cup confectioners' sugar

2 cups heavy (whipping) cream

¾ cup Baileys Irish Cream liqueur

One ¼-ounce envelope unflavored gelatin

1 cup boiling water

Fresh berries for garnish

1 **To make the crust:** Preheat the oven to 350°F. In a small bowl, combine the crumbs and melted butter. Press the crumb mixture onto the bottom and up the sides of a 9-inch round springform pan. Bake for 8 to 10 minutes, or until lightly browned. Remove from the oven and let cool on a wire rack.

CONTINUED

2   **To make the syrup:** In a medium saucepan over medium heat, combine the stout and brown sugar. Gently bring to a boil, then reduce the heat to low and simmer for 8 to 10 minutes, or until the mixture is thick and syrupy and coats the back of a spoon. Remove from the heat and let cool.

3   **To make the filling:** In a large bowl, combine the cream cheese and confectioners' sugar and beat until smooth with an electric mixer. Add the cream and beat for 3 to 4 minutes, or until smooth. Stir in half the Murphy's syrup and all of the Baileys. In a small bowl, combine the gelatin and boiling water. Stir until the gelatin is completely dissolved, about 5 minutes. Stir 2 tablespoons of the syrup into the gelatin, then stir the gelatin into the cream cheese mixture. Pour the filling over the biscuit crust. Refrigerate for 3 to 4 hours, or until firm. Set aside the remaining syrup at room temperature.

4   When ready to serve, release the sides of the pan and cut the cheesecake into wedges. Drizzle some of the remaining Murphy's syrup around each slice and garnish with fresh berries.

GUINNESS STOREHOUSE

First opened in November 2000, the Guinness Storehouse is based in the heart of the St. James's Gate Brewery in Dublin, where millions of gallons of Guinness stout are brewed each year. St. James's Gate is the biggest stout brewery in the world. The building itself was built in 1904, and was the first steel-framed building in Ireland. One of the highlights of the building, spread out over about four acres, is its seven-story glass atrium, cleverly designed in the shape of a pint glass. Glass-walled elevators bring visitors on a delightful journey through the past, present, and future of one of the world's greatest beers. Floor by floor, the ingredients, process, time, craft, and passion that goes into every pint is revealed.

Ten million glasses of Guinness are consumed daily in more than 150 countries worldwide, and in Ireland, one in every two pints consumed is Guinness. So it would be hard to find a more perfect place to enjoy a pint than in the Gravity Bar, the end of the tour for visitors to the Storehouse. There you will find an expert barman who gives full attention to the angle at which the glass is held, the speed of the pour, the time given for the pint to settle, and the moment chosen for the top off—matters of great importance to Guinness drinkers. Located eight feet above the roof line, the Gravity Bar is the highest in Dublin. While relaxing with your complimentary pint, you can enjoy an uninterrupted 360-degree panoramic view of Dublin and its surroundings, from the Phoenix Park down the River Liffey to Dublin Bay and the Wicklow Mountains. Since its opening, the Storehouse has hosted 2 million visitors and is currently the number-one visitor attraction in the country. For details, see Resources, page 214.

Sheila Sharpe, one of Ireland's foremost pastry chefs, is in charge of the sweet side of the Oarsman, a delightful pub-restaurant in the heart of Carrick-on-Shannon, in County Leitrim. Established in 1879, the attractive pub has plenty of Old World charm: a warm atmosphere, stone fireplaces, and original pitch pine floors. Under the ownership of Conor and Ronan Maher, seventh-generation hoteliers and publicans, the Oarsman is a pleasant mix of traditional Irish style and contemporary Irish cooking. This marbled chocolate mousse cake is a perfect example. SERVES 8

MARBLED CHOCOLATE MOUSSE CAKE

CAKE

4 ounces semisweet or bittersweet chocolate

3 large eggs

½ cup sugar

½ cup all-purpose flour

MOUSSE

4 ounces white chocolate

Two ¼-ounce packages unflavored gelatin

3 tablespoons hot water

3 large eggs, separated

3 tablespoons Baileys Irish Cream liqueur

6 ounces semisweet or bittersweet chocolate

¼ cup Irish Mist, heated

2 cups heavy (whipping) cream

Fresh strawberries for garnish (optional)

1   **To make the cake:** Preheat the oven to 300°F. Butter a 9-inch springform pan.

2   In a small saucepan over medium-low heat, melt the semisweet or bittersweet chocolate. In a large bowl, beat the eggs and sugar with an electric mixer for 4 to 5 minutes, or until light and fluffy. Beat in the melted chocolate and the flour. Spread the mixture into the prepared pan and bake for 15 to 18 minutes, or until the top springs back when lightly touched. Remove from the oven and let cool completely in the pan on a wire rack.

3   **To make the mousse:** In a small saucepan over medium-low heat, melt the white chocolate. Sprinkle 1 package of the gelatin over the hot water and stir until completely dissolved. Whisk 1 egg yolk into the white chocolate. Stir in the gelatin mixture and the Baileys Irish Cream.

4   In a small saucepan over medium-low heat, melt the semisweet or bittersweet chocolate. Sprinkle the remaining package of gelatin over the Irish Mist, and stir until completely dissolved. Whisk the remaining 2 egg yolks into the dark chocolate. Stir in the gelatin mixture.

5   Whip the cream in a medium bowl with an electric mixer until stiff peaks form. Fold two thirds of the cream into the dark chocolate mixture and one third into the white chocolate mixture. With clean beaters, whip the egg whites in a medium bowl with an electric mixer until stiff peaks form. Fold two thirds of the whites into the dark chocolate mixture and one third into the white chocolate mixture.

6   Spoon the dark chocolate mousse over the cake and spread to cover. Spoon the white chocolate mousse over the top. Using the point of a small knife, move it through the two mousse mixtures to create a marbled effect. Refrigerate for at least 2 hours, or until the mousse is firm.

7   When ready to serve, release the sides of the pan and cut the cake into wedges. Garnish with some fresh berries, if desired.

•••••

FOLLOWING PAGES: AN TEACH BEAG, CLONAKILTY, COUNTY CORK

Did you ever hear tell of Matt the Thresher, a man who had a penchant for perfection and a prowess known far and wide? "Sure, there's nothing could beat Matt the Thresher" became a well-known saying in bygone days, especially in the area of Birdhill, County Tipperary, on the borders of Counties Clare and Limerick. Today Birdhill is the site of a pub, restaurant, and guesthouse named for the illustrious Matt, all of which are under the direction of the Moynihan family. With Kay Moynihan in charge of the kitchen, Matt the Thresher is consistently ranked among the finest pubs in Ireland and the UK. Many think there's nothing that can beat Kay's Irish chocolate cake. **SERVES 8**

IRISH CHOCOLATE CAKE
with Buttercream Icing

CAKE

2½ cups self-rising flour

2 tablespoons cocoa

6 ounces semisweet chocolate, grated

1½ cups (3 sticks) unsalted Kerrygold Irish butter at room temperature

1½ cups superfine sugar

6 large eggs, beaten

BUTTERCREAM

1½ cups unsalted Kerrygold Irish butter at room temperature

3 cups confectioners' sugar

½ cup cocoa

¶ **To make the cake:** Preheat the oven to 350°F. Line the bottom of a 10-inch round baking pan with lightly greased wax paper and grease the sides of the pan.

2 In a large bowl, sift together the flour and cocoa. Set aside. In a small saucepan over medium-low heat, melt the chocolate. In a large bowl, beat the butter and sugar with an electric mixer for 4 to 5 minutes, or until light and fluffy. Beat in the eggs, one at a time, then fold in the flour mixture and melted chocolate.

3 Pour the batter into the prepared pan and bake for about 1 hour and 10 minutes, or until a skewer inserted in the center comes out clean. Remove the cake from the oven and let cool in the pan for 10 minutes. Invert the cake onto a wire rack, remove the wax paper, and reinvert to cool completely. When cool, cut the cake horizontally into 2 layers.

4 **To make the buttercream:** In a large bowl beat the butter and sugar with an electric mixer for 3 to 4 minutes, or until light and fluffy. Beat in the cocoa.

5 With a spatula, spread half of the buttercream onto the cut side of the bottom layer. Place the other layer on top, and spread the top and sides with the remaining buttercream. Let the icing set for 15 to 20 minutes before cutting the cake into slices.

Keenans is situated in the picturesque village of Tarmonbarry, County Roscommon, on the banks of the river Shannon. Established around 1860, the pub is currently operated by Barry and Annette Keenan, fifth-generation proprietors. The pub has evolved over the years, with each generation making its own stamp; the menu changes to keep up with current trends. Tarmonbarry itself is a great place to visit, with many attractions nearby, including Lough Rinn House and Gardens, Strokestown House, Carriglas Manor, Lough Key Forest Park, and, of course, great fishing and boating on the Shannon. Since many European visitors spend holidays on river cruisers, the pub offers a wide selection of continental dishes, as well as traditional Irish desserts like this delightful crumble baked in a cookie dough-like base. Keenans is a member of Irish Pubs of Distinction (see page 159), and was named County Roscommon "Pub of the Year" in the 2004 Black and White pub awards competition (see page 111).

SERVES 6 TO 8

APPLE-BERRY CRUMBLE

CRUST

1½ cups all-purpose flour

2 tablespoons sugar

½ cup (1 stick) cold unsalted Kerrygold Irish butter, cut into small pieces

1 large egg yolk

2 to 3 tablespoons ice water

FILLING

2 Granny Smith apples, peeled, cored, and sliced

2 cups mixed berries, such as blackberries, raspberries, and blueberries

2 tablespoons confectioners' sugar

2 tablespoons cornstarch

TOPPING

1 cup all-purpose flour

½ cup light brown sugar

½ cup Irish oatmeal, preferably McCann's brand

1 cup (2 sticks) cold unsalted Kerrygold Irish butter, cut into small pieces

¼ cup sliced almonds

Whipped cream for serving

1   **To make the crust:** Butter an 11-inch tart pan with a removable bottom. Combine the flour, sugar, and butter in a food processor fitted with a metal blade. Pulse 8 to 10 times, or until the mixture resembles coarse crumbs. Add the egg and 2 tablespoons of the water and process for 15 to 20 seconds, or until the dough comes together. Add the additional 1 tablespoon of water if the dough seems too dry. Transfer the dough to the prepared pan and press it onto the bottom and up the sides. Refrigerate for 30 minutes.

2   Preheat the oven to 350°F.

3   **To make the filling:** Layer the apples into the crust and top with the berries. In a small bowl, combine the confectioners' sugar and cornstarch and sprinkle over the berries.

4   **To make the topping:** In a small bowl, combine the flour, brown sugar, oatmeal, and butter. With a pastry cutter or 2 knives, blend until the mixture resembles coarse crumbs. Stir in the almonds, and sprinkle the mixture over the fruit.

5   Bake the crumble for 40 to 45 minutes, or until the topping is golden and the fruit is bubbling. Remove from the oven and let cool on a wire rack for about 10 minutes. Serve warm with whipped cream.

Croom Mills is a vibrant, fully operational corn-grinding mill located on the banks of the River Maigue in Croom, County Limerick. It is thought to be one of the finest grain mill restoration projects in Ireland. The visitor center not only pays tribute to an era of country life in Ireland's Golden Vale, but it also houses two restaurants, the Mill Race and Harvest Restaurant, and has recently added a pub, the Miller's Inn, which serves snacks, light food, and delicious desserts like this tart made with pears and almonds. The recommended accompaniment: a generous scoop of freshly whipped cream. **SERVES 8 TO 10**

PEAR AND ALMOND TART

CRUST

1¾ cups all-purpose flour

½ cup (1 stick) cold unsalted Kerrygold Irish butter, cut into small pieces

1 tablespoon sugar

2 large eggs

4 to 5 tablespoons ice water

FILLING

½ cup (1 stick) unsalted Kerrygold Irish butter at room temperature

½ cup sugar

2 large eggs

½ cup finely ground almonds

2 teaspoons all-purpose flour

½ teaspoon almond extract

⅓ cup apricot preserves

2 firm-ripe Bartlett or Anjou pears, peeled, cored, and cut into ¼-inch slices

Whipped cream for serving (optional)

1   **To start the crust:** Combine the flour, butter, and sugar in a food processor fitted with a metal blade. Pulse 8 to 10 times, or until the mixture resembles coarse crumbs. Add the eggs and 4 tablespoons of the water, and process for 15 to 20 seconds, or until the dough comes together. Add the remaining tablespoon of water if necessary. Turn out the dough on a work surface, form it into a ball, and wrap in plastic wrap. Refrigerate for 1 hour. Remove the dough from the refrigerator 10 minutes before rolling.

2   Preheat the oven to 350°F.

3   **To start the filling:** Cream the butter and sugar together in a medium bowl with an electric mixer. Beat in the eggs, one at a time, then the almonds, flour, and almond extract.

4   Butter a 10-inch tart pan with a removable bottom. Dust a work surface with flour. Roll out the dough to a circle 12 inches in diameter. Transfer to the prepared pan, fold in the excess dough, and press with your fingers to form thick sides. In a small saucepan or in a microwave oven, heat the apricot preserves until runny. Spread the preserves over the crust.

5   Pour the custard into the crust. Starting in the center, arrange the pear slices in concentric circles over the custard. Bake for 35 to 40 minutes, or until the custard is puffed and browned and the pears are tender. Remove from the oven and transfer to a wire rack. Cool the tart in the pan completely before releasing the side. Serve with whipped cream, if desired.

VARIATION:
Bakewell Tart

In the pub and restaurant at O'Donovan's Hotel in Clonakilty, County Cork, chef Angela Brennan calls a similar recipe a Bakewell Tart. Legend has it that the original Bakewell tart was the result of a mistake made by the cook at the Rutland Arms in Bakewell (Derbyshire, England), who, instead of adding butter, eggs, and sugar to the pastry, made them into a filling instead. Follow the recipe as described above, substituting raspberry jam for the apricot preserves and omitting the ground almonds and pears. When the tart is cool, sprinkle the top with confectioners' sugar.

• • • • •
FOLLOWING PAGES: THE MILLER'S INN AT CROOM MILLS, CROOM, COUNTY LIMERICK

Bread and butter pudding is one of the most popular desserts served in Ireland. For a dish with such universal appeal, it's surprising to find that each recipe—whether it's from Moone High Cross Inn in County Kildare, An Súgán in County Cork, or Davy Byrnes in Dublin—has its own unique method of preparation or unusual ingredient. This, however, is my favorite. The hot whiskey sauce is a welcome alternative to the traditional custard sauce. **SERVES 6 TO 8; MAKES ABOUT 1 CUP OF SAUCE**

BREAD AND BUTTER PUDDING
with Hot Whiskey Sauce

PUDDING

½ cup raisins

½ cup Irish whiskey

5 large eggs

2 cups heavy (whipping) cream

1 cup sugar

½ teaspoon ground cinnamon

¼ teaspoon ground nutmeg

1 teaspoon vanilla extract

8 ounces (8 to 9 slices) firm white bread, crust left on

4 tablespoons unsalted Kerrygold Irish butter at room temperature

HOT WHISKEY SAUCE

½ cup (1 stick) unsalted Kerrygold Irish butter, cut into pieces

1 cup sugar

6 tablespoons heavy (whipping) cream

¼ cup Irish whiskey

1. **To make the pudding:** In a small bowl, combine the raisins and whiskey and let soak for 1 hour. Butter a 9-inch square nonreactive baking dish.

2. In a large bowl, whisk together the eggs, cream, sugar, cinnamon, nutmeg, and vanilla. Spread one side of each slice of bread with butter. Cut the slices in half diagonally and arrange half the bread in the bottom of the baking dish, overlapping the slices. Drain the raisins and sprinkle half over the bread. Repeat with the remaining bread and raisins. Pour the custard over the bread and let it soak for 30 minutes.

3. Preheat the oven to 400°F. Place the baking dish in a large baking pan. Add enough hot water to come halfway up the sides of the dish. Bake for 50 to 60 minutes, or until the pudding is set and the top is golden. Remove the baking dish from the water bath and let cool slightly on a wire rack.

4. **To make the whiskey sauce:** In a small saucepan over medium heat, melt the butter. Whisk in the sugar, cream, and whiskey. Reduce the heat to low and simmer for 4 to 5 minutes, or until the sauce thickens. Serve the pudding warm with the whiskey sauce spooned over each portion.

The Guinness Storehouse, at St. James's Gate in Dublin (see page 191), is currently Ireland's number-one international visitor attraction. Its Brewery Bar, a full service pub-restaurant, is the perfect place for lunch or dinner, or to kick back for a drink after touring the incredible facility. Guinness's renowned stout is a surprisingly sweet addition to a chocolate mousse, like this one served at the Storehouse. Top it with a white chocolate mousse for a look-alike of a creamy pint. **SERVES 8**

Guinness Black and White
CHOCOLATE MOUSSE

BLACK CHOCOLATE MOUSSE

8 ounces semisweet or bittersweet chocolate, chopped or grated

½ cup (1 stick) unsalted Kerrygold Irish butter

¼ cup superfine sugar

¾ cup Guinness stout

3 large eggs, separated

1 cup heavy (whipping) cream

WHITE CHOCOLATE MOUSSE

6 ounces white chocolate, chopped or grated

1 cup heavy (whipping) cream

1   **To make the black chocolate mousse:** In a small bowl set over a pan of simmering water, or in a double boiler, combine the chocolate, butter, and sugar. Stir until the chocolate has melted and the mixture is smooth. Stir in the Guinness and whisk in the egg yolks. Remove from the heat.

2   In a small bowl, whip the cream with an electric mixer until soft peaks form. Fold the cream into the chocolate mixture. With clean beaters, in a medium bowl, beat the egg whites with an electric mixer until stiff peaks form. Fold the whites into the chocolate mixture. Fill 8 wine or parfait glasses three quarters full with the chocolate mixture. Refrigerate while preparing the white chocolate mousse.

3   **To make the white chocolate mousse:** In a small saucepan over medium heat, combine the white chocolate and ¹/₂ cup of the cream. Stir until the chocolate has melted and the mixture is smooth. Remove from the heat and let cool, stirring once or twice, for 30 minutes, or until thickened. In a small bowl, beat the remaining ¹/₂ cup of cream with an electric mixer until stiff peaks form. Fold the whipped cream into the white chocolate mixture. Spoon the mixture over the top of the chocolate mousses and refrigerate for at least 2, and up to 24, hours.

The building that houses McHugh's, on Queens Square in Belfast, is the oldest in the city. Located in the dock area under the gaze of the Albert Clock and adjacent to the River Lagan, McHugh's is an integral piece of Belfast's current and future revitalization. The Prince's Street entrance opens into a dramatic gallery with massive eighteenth-century oak trusses, while a restored ship boiler embedded in the walls warms the area. The bar-restaurant prides itself on a reputation of good food, entertainment, and atmosphere, giving McHugh's the enviable title of "the best little ale house" in Belfast. McHugh's is also included on the historical pub crawl of Belfast sponsored by Baileys Irish Cream (see page 144). A glass of the creamy whiskey-based liqueur would make a decadent accompaniment to this rich banana-laden toffee pie, known as "banoffe." McHugh's is a member of Irish Pubs of Distinction (see page 159). **SERVES 8 TO 10.**

BANOFFE PIE

CRUMB CRUST

1 cup crumbs from Irish digestive biscuits, such as Carr's or McVitie's brand (6 to 8 biscuits)

3 tablespoons unsalted Kerrygold Irish butter, melted

FILLING

1 can sweetened condensed milk (not evaporated milk), such as Eagle brand

2 bananas, peeled and sliced

Crème fraîche (see page 46) or whipped cream for topping

1   **To make the crust:** Preheat the oven to 350°F. In a small bowl, combine the crumbs and melted butter. Press the crumb mixture onto the bottom of a 10-inch round quiche pan or tart pan with a removable bottom. Bake for 8 to 10 minutes, or until lightly browned. Remove from the oven and let cool on a wire rack.

2   **To make the filling:** Pour the sweetened condensed milk into a 2-quart glass microwavable bowl. Microwave on 50 percent power (Medium) for 4 minutes, stirring after 2 minutes. Reduce to 30 percent power (Low) and microwave for 12 to 16 minutes, stirring briskly every 2 minutes, or until the mixture is thick and toffee-colored. Remove from the microwave and let cool slightly. Alternatively, put the sweetened condensed milk into the top of a double boiler set over boiling water. Over low heat, cook, covered, for 1 to 1 1/2 hours, or until thick and toffee-colored. Beat until smooth.

3   Arrange the sliced bananas in concentric circles over the crumb crust. Spread the toffee over the bananas and let the toffee set for 30 minutes.

4   To serve, cut the pie into wedges and top each slice with crème fraîche or whipped cream.

VARIATION:

Strawberry-Raspberry Banoffe Pie

At Johnnie Fox's Pub, in Glencullen, County Dublin, the chef uses raspberries in his banoffe pie, which he says "grow as big as strawberries." Since most raspberries aren't this large, I've added strawberries as well; the two are a pleasant alternative to bananas. Prepare the crumb crust and toffee as described in the recipe. Spread the toffee over the crust. Whip 2 cups of heavy cream with an electric mixer until stiff peaks form. Spread it over the toffee. Hull 1½ pints (about 20) strawberries. Starting in the center, stand the strawberries up in concentric circles over the whipped cream. Place the ½ pint of raspberries in between the strawberries. In a microwave oven, heat half a 10-ounce jar of apricot preserves with 1 tablespoon of water for 20 to 30 seconds, or until runny. Let cool for 5 minutes, then spoon over the strawberries and raspberries to glaze the fruit. Refrigerate for at least 1 hour.

O'Sullivan's Thatch, located halfway between Ballybunion and Listowel, in County Kerry, has been in the O'Sullivan family for four generations. The exterior is original thatch, and inside is a handsome pub and restaurant with timber columns, cottage windows, and a big granite fireplace. Maurice Walsh, author of the book that inspired the famous movie *The Quiet Man,* lived next door, and the Thatch was his local watering hole. Under the current owners, Eugene and Lucille O'Sullivan, the pub continues to thrive as a venue for lively music, impromptu sessions, and good food, such as this yummy frozen terrine made with white chocolate and topped with ladyfingers, known in Ireland as "trifle sponges." **SERVES 8**

BLACKBOARD SPECIAL

WHITE CHOCOLATE TERRINE

6 large eggs, separated

¾ cups superfine sugar

½ teaspoon vanilla extract

2 cups milk

2 cups heavy (whipping) cream

8 ounces white chocolate, chopped

One ¼-ounce envelope unflavored gelatin

¼ cup water

8 ladyfingers or trifle sponges

Fresh strawberries, hulled and halved, for garnish

1   Line a 9-by-3-by-5-inch loaf pan with wax paper.

2   In a medium bowl, combine the egg yolks and sugar and beat with an electric mixer until light and fluffy. Whisk in the vanilla and set aside.

3   In a medium saucepan over medium heat, combine the milk and cream. Bring slowly to a boil. Gradually whisk the milk mixture into the yolk mixture, then return to the saucepan. Stir in the white chocolate and whisk until smooth. Remove from the heat and let cool for at least 1 hour, stirring frequently to prevent a skin from forming.

4   In a small saucepan, sprinkle the gelatin over the water. Let stand for 1 to 2 minutes, then heat gently for 2 to 3 minutes, or until the gelatin dissolves. Set aside.

5   With clean beaters, in a medium bowl, beat the egg whites with an electric mixer until stiff peaks form. Fold the whites into the white chocolate mixture. Fold in the gelatin mixture. Pour into the prepared pan and arrange the ladyfingers side-by-side over the top. Freeze for 4 to 6 hours, or until firm.

6   To serve, invert the loaf pan onto a serving plate, remove the wax paper, then reinvert so it is right side up. Cut it into slices between each of the ladyfingers, and garnish with strawberries.

 ## SWEET IRISH CREAMS

Irish cream liqueurs are made from a blend of two of Ireland's greatest treasures: the cream from its rich dairy pastures and the spirits from its finest distilleries. Baileys Irish Cream, the first of the bunch, was launched in 1974, after the company discovered the secret that would prevent cream from separating after being blended with neutral spirits, Irish whiskey, and natural flavors. Steeped in Irish history and lore, the drink was named after a Dublin pub called the Bailey, a favorite haunt of James Joyce. The bottle design is based on an old Irish whiskey brand, Red Breast.

Some say that a whiskey-flavored cream like Baileys is based on a west of Ireland tradition of stirring fresh cream into Irish whiskey for sipping. Baileys' popularity has spread throughout Ireland and the world. Today there are several brands of Irish cream liqueur, including Carolan's, Emmet's, Saint Brendan's, O'Mara's, Bushmills, and Brady's. The last is a newcomer made in a small-batch process and bottled within forty-eight hours of the cream reaching the distillery. Unlike many Irish creams, Brady's is made with Irish single malt whiskey as well as neutral grain spirits. Its natural flavors of dark chocolate and vanilla give it a distinctly lush, full taste. Irish cream liqueurs, available in the United States and elsewhere, are a perfect ingredient in desserts ranging from cheesecake to chocolate mousse to ice cream.

ARUGULA

Also known as "rocket," arugula is a bitter, peppery green often associated with Italian cooking. It's a popular salad ingredient in Ireland.

BACON

Traditional Irish bacon is available in a number of cuts, including the shoulder or collar (also called "boiling bacon"), loin (most often used for chops), streaky (also known as "rashers" and served as part of an Irish breakfast), and gammon (also known as "ham").

BANGERS

Bangers are sausages made of ground pork and bread crumbs. They are used in Coddle (page 100), and are served as part of an Irish breakfast or with mashed potatoes for dinner.

BLACK PUDDING

Black pudding is a sausage made of ground pork, spices, oatmeal, and pork blood, which gives the pudding its distinctive color. It is traditionally served as part of an Irish breakfast, although today it is also used as an ingredient in salads, meat dishes, and risottos. Clonakilty, County Cork, is known for its fine black pudding.

BLUE CHEESE

There are several types of farm house blue cheese produced in Ireland: Cashel Blue is made in Fethard, County Tipperary, by the Grubb family from the milk of pedigreed Friesian cows; Crozier Blue, also from the Grubb family, is made from sheep's milk; and Bellingham Blue, another cow's milk cheese, is made by Peter Thomas in Castlebellingham, County Louth; Kerrygold, a commercial producer of cheeses, recently launched Kerrygold Blue.

BOUILLON

Also called "stock" or "broth," bouillon is the liquid that is drained off after cooking meat, poultry, fish, or vegetables. It is used in soups and sauces. Concentrated bouillon is sold in cubes and granules and must be dissolved in hot liquid before it is added to soups and stews. Popular brands are Knorr, Maggi, and Goya. Oxo is a well-known brand in Ireland.

BOUQUET GARNI

A mixture of herbs tied in a cheesecloth bag. It's used to flavor soups and stews.

CAMEMBERT CHEESE

This world-famous cow's milk cheese is named for a Norman village in France. It has a white rind and creamy interior. In Ireland, there are several farmhouse cheese makers who produce this style of cheese, including Carrigbyrne Farmhouse's St. Killian and Cooleeney.

Courgette

In Ireland, zucchini squash is called by this French name.

Irish Cream Liqueurs

Made from Irish whiskey, double cream, neutral spirits, and natural flavors, Irish cream liqueurs are frequently used in Irish cooking, especially for desserts. Baileys Irish Cream was the first one.

Poitín

Distilled from barley, sugar, and water, poitín was originally made in pot stills over a peat fire. It was banned in Ireland in 1661 and was only recently legalized. Bunratty Poitín (also known as "potcheen") is now sold throughout the country as well as in the United States. This clear liquid is sometimes used as a substitute for Irish whiskey. Another brand to look for is Knockeen Hills.

Pork. See *Bacon, Bangers, and Black Pudding*

Porter. See *Stout*

Stout

A strong, dark beer made with hops and dark-roasted barley. Guinness and Murphy's are Ireland's most popular stouts. The brew was originally called "porter," but Arthur Guinness renamed the beer "stout" for its strong, bold taste.

Tian

A tian is a shallow casserole dish as well as the food that it contains. A ring mold is sometimes used to create a tian.

Vol-au-vent

A vol-au-vent is a small, cup-shaped puff pastry shell with a lid. It is generally filled with a cream sauce-based mixture of meat, seafood, or vegetables and baked. It can also be filled with fruit, ice cream, or pudding for dessert. Pepperidge Farms makes frozen pastry shells that can be used for vol-au-vents.

Whole-wheat flour

"Whole-meal flour" is the Irish name for whole-wheat flour, an important ingredient in Irish soda bread. To obtain the best texture, use extra-coarse whole-meal flour such as Odlums or Howard's brand (see Resources, page 214).

RESOURCES

Use this guide to find food and beverages from Ireland, ingredients called for in some recipes, or locations and events mentioned in this book.

To find an Irish shop in your area where some of these products are available, contact Enterprise Ireland, 345 Park Avenue, New York, NY 10154; phone 212-371-3600. Or try Bord Bia, the Irish Food Board, 400 North Michigan Avenue, Chicago, IL 60611; phone 773-871-6749, or visit www.bordbia.ie.

For information on travel to Ireland, including accommodations, culture, sports, and festivals, contact Tourism Ireland, 345 Park Avenue, New York, NY 10154; phone 800-223-6470, or visit www.tourismireland.com.

For information on a specific region of Ireland, visit www.corkkerry.ie for counties Cork and Kerry; www.visitdublin.com for Dublin city and county; www.ecoast-midlands.travel.ie for counties Kildare, Laois, Longford, Louth, Meath, North Offaly, Westmeath, and Wicklow; www.irelandnorthwest.ie for counties Cavan, Donegal, Leitrim, Monaghan, and Sligo; www.irelandwest.ie for counties Galway, Mayo, and Roscommon; www.shannonregiontourism.ie for counties Clare, Limerick, North Kerry, North Tipperary, and South Offaly; www.southeastireland.com for counties Carlow, Kildare, Tipperary, Waterford, and Wexford; www.discovernorthernireland.com for counties Antrim, Armagh, Derry, Down, Fermanagh, and Tyrone.

BACON

Depending on the cut of bacon required, traditional Irish bacon and ham can be found in many Irish butcher shops as well as from specialty grocers in the U.S. Contact Traditional Irish Foods, phone 877-474-7436, or visit www.foodireland.com; Irish Grub, www.irishgrub.com; Schaller and Weber, phone 212-879-3047, or visit www.schallerweber.com.

BANTRY BAY MUSSEL FESTIVAL

This festival is held each May in the seaside town of Bantry, in County Cork. For details, contact the Bantry Tourist Office; phone 011-353-27-50229, or visit www.corkkerry.ie.

BELFAST HISTORICAL PUB CRAWL

Baileys Irish Cream sponsors this tour of historic Belfast pubs. A professional guide, who provides both history and humor along the way, leads the tour. For details, contact the Belfast Tourist Office, 47 Donegall Place, Belfast; phone 011-44-28-9024-6609, or visit www.gotobelfast.com.

BLACK AND WHITE PUB AWARDS

These awards, sponsored by Edward Dillon and Company, Dublin, honor Ireland's top regional pubs. To find out this year's winners, visit www.edwarddillonco.ie.

BLOOMSDAY

June 16 is "Bloomsday," the day James Joyce's novel *Ulysses* takes place. For information on annual events in Dublin, contact the James Joyce Centre, 35 North Great George's Street, Dublin; or visit www.jamesjoyce.ie.

BUTTER AND CHEESE

To find out what supermarkets sell Kerrygold Irish butter and cheeses, contact the Irish Dairy Board U.S.A.; phone 847-256-8289, or visit www.idbusa.com. To buy Kerrygold products, contact Traditional Irish Foods; phone 877-474-7436, or visit www.foodireland.com.

To buy imported Irish farmhouse cheeses in the U.S., such as Cooleeney, Cashel Blue, St. Tola, and Carrigbyrne's St. Killian, contact Murray's Cheese Shop; phone 888-692-4339, or visit www.murrayscheese.com.

CLARENBRIDGE OYSTER FESTIVAL

This rollicking festival is held annually in the village of Clarenbridge, in County Galway, to celebrate the return of native oysters in September. For details on the event, visit www.clarenbridgefestival.com or www.irelandwest.ie.

CROWN SALOON

The British National Trust has owned one of Ireland's Victorian pubs, the Crown, since 1978. This popular tourist venue in Belfast receives thousands of visitors from around the world each year (see pages 128 and 131). Visit www.crownbar.com.

DUBLIN LITERARY PUB CRAWL

A lively, animated evening of literature and laughs from professional actors who perform passages from the works of well-known Dublin literary figures, such as James Joyce and Brendan Behan, as you quench your thirst in several pubs around the city. For details, visit www.dublinpubcrawl.com.

DUBLIN MUSICAL PUB CRAWL

Led by two professional musicians, the tour takes you to several pubs in Dublin's Temple Bar area and gives you an opportunity to participate in song while you down a few pints and learn the story of Irish music. For details, visit www.musicalpubcrawl.com.

Galway Oyster Festival

This world-class homage to oysters is held each September in the city of Galway. For details, visit www.galwayoysterfest.com, or www.irelandwest.ie.

Guinness Storehouse

Ireland's number-one paid visitor attraction, the Guinness Storehouse is a contemporary "museum" devoted to the history and production of Guinness stout, one of Ireland's most popular drinks. Visit www.guinness.com.

Irish Pub Company

The Dublin-based architectural and design company McNally Design Group is the parent group of the Irish Pub Company. They design and construct authentic Irish pubs around the world. Visit www.irishpubcompany.com.

Irish Pubs of Distinction

To obtain a copy of the Irish Pubs of Distinction brochure, which lists member pubs by county, visit the Vintners Federation of Ireland at www.vfi.ie or www.pubireland.net.

Lakeshore Whole-grain Mustard

To order Lakeshore mustard in the U.S., contact Bewley Irish Imports; phone 800-BEWLEY, or visit www.bewleyirishimports.com.

Oatmeal

McCann's brand Irish oatmeal is available in most supermarkets. McCann's, Flahavans, and Odlums brands are available from Traditional Irish Foods; phone 877-474-7436, or visit www.foodireland.com.

Poitín

To find out where you can buy authentic poitín (bottled as Bunratty Potcheen), contact Camelot Importing Co.; phone 800-4-CAMELOT.

Smoked Salmon

Some brands of oak-smoked Irish salmon are available from Traditional Irish Foods; phone 877-474-7436, or visit www.foodireland.com.

Stove-top Smoker

Cameron's Professional Cookware makes a stove-top smoker that can be used to smoke poultry, fish, meats, and vegetables. For details, visit www.cameronscookware.com.

Whole-wheat Flour

Irish whole-wheat flour, such as Odlums and Howard's brands, is available from Traditional Irish Foods; phone 877-474-7436, or visit www.foodireland.com.

The exact equivalents in the following tables have been rounded for convenience.

Liquid/Dry Measures

U.S.	Metric
¼ teaspoon	1.25 milliliters
½ teaspoon	2.5 milliliters
1 teaspoon	5 milliliters
1 tablespoon (3 teaspoons)	15 milliliters
1 fluid ounce (2 tablespoons)	30 milliliters
¼ cup	60 milliliters
⅓ cup	80 milliliters
½ cup	120 milliliters
1 cup	240 milliliters
1 pint (2 cups)	480 milliliters
1 quart (4 cups, 32 ounces)	960 milliliters
1 gallon (4 quarts)	3.84 liters
1 ounce (by weight)	28 grams
1 pound	454 grams
2.2 pounds	1 kilogram

Length

U.S.	Metric
⅛ inch	3 millimeters
¼ inch	6 millimeters
½ inch	12 millimeters
1 inch	2.5 centimeters

Oven Temperature

Fahrenheit	Celsius	Gas
250	120	½
275	140	1
300	150	2
325	160	3
350	180	4
375	190	5
400	200	6
425	220	7
450	230	8
475	240	9
500	260	10